Ferdinand Hahn

The Worship
of the Early Church

Translated by DAVID E. GREEN

Edited, with an Introduction, by

JOHN REUMANN

FORTRESS PRESS   Philadelphia

This book is a translation of "Der urchristliche Gottesdienst," which appeared originally in the *Jahrbuch für Liturgik und Hymnologie*, edited by Konrad Ameln, Christhard Mahrenholz, and Karl Ferdinand Müller, Volume 12 (1967), pp. 1–44, published by Johannes Stauda-Verlag, Kassel, 1968; reprinted with corrections and bibliographical additions as *Der urchristliche Gottesdienst*, Stuttgarter Bibelstudien 41, edited by Herbert Haag, Rudolf Kilian, and Wilhelm Pesch (Stuttgart: Verlag Katholisches Bibelwerk, 1970). It is translated here by arrangement with Johannes Stauda-Verlag, Kassel, and Verlag Katholisches Bibelwerk, Stuttgart.

Library of Congress Catalog Card Number 72-87063
ISBN 0-8006-0127-0

Third printing 1980

8861J80   Printed in the United States of America   1–127

Contents

Editor's Introduction

Professor Ferdinand Hahn's panoramic survey of the worship of the early church—concentrating on the New Testament but with attention to Old Testament and Jewish backgrounds and to the decisive attitudes of Jesus himself, and with a look also on into the second Christian century—has scarcely received the recognition it deserves. Yet it is a comprehensive analysis, bringing order out of a topic where there has been a considerable amount of literature in recent years but nothing quite so succinct as this essay.

There are factors explaining why this study has not become widely known since it first appeared in 1967. Though the work of a ranking New Testament scholar, it was published originally in an annual designed for experts in liturgics, the German *Jahrbuch für Liturgik und Hymnologie* (12 [1967]: 1–44), a publication which, by the way, students of the Bible might do well to note because of its bibliographical riches and occasional major articles on scripture. It was then reprinted, with slight revision—even though the author is an Evangelical churchman and teaches in a Protestant theological faculty—as Volume 41 (1970) in a Catholic monograph series which seeks to popularize scriptural research, the Stuttgarter Bibelstudien (Stuttgart: Verlag Katholisches Bibelwerk). Such an ecumenical, interdisciplinary background gives good reason for providing the English translation offered here for the first time, as do the excellence of the contents and need for such a brief survey.

The author is Professor of New Testament in the Evangelical Theological Faculty at Johannes-Gutenberg-University in Mainz, Germany (where, since its establishment in 1946, there has also been side by side a Catholic theological faculty). He has been hailed for writing the most important doctoral dissertation in New Testament studies at a German university since the Second World War, a work on Christology which has been claimed by some to be *the* treatment on the subject by present-day German scholarship.

Ferdinand Hahn was born in 1926 at Kaiserslautern (Pfalz) and studied theology between 1947 and 1953 at the universities in Mainz, Göttingen, and Heidelberg, concentrating on New Testament studies, especially under Ernst Käsemann and Günther Bornkamm. In 1956, after service as a minister in the Evangelical Church, he returned to Heidelberg as assistant to Professor Bornkamm. There he completed his doctoral studies and the preparation of the dissertation on christological titles (1961) and the second dissertation (Habilitationsschrift) which marks one for a teaching position in the German university system; this second study, completed in 1962–63, was concerned with how Christians of the New Testament period understood the concept of mission and spoke of the church's missionary task.

Dr. Hahn's dissertation was promptly published in

1963 in the prestigious series, Forschungen zur Religion und Literatur des Alten und Neuen Testaments,
and his further study, *Das Verständnis der Mission im
Neuen Testament,* was printed the same year in another important series of monographs. In 1964 Dr.
Hahn became professor in the University at Kiel;
from there he moved to Mainz in 1968. The book on
"mission" was translated in the series Studies in
Biblical Theology in 1965, and the earlier, larger
work on "titles of christological exaltation" was published in English in 1969. These two major works
enabled him, as it were, to burst upon the world of
New Testament scholarship as few other scholars have
done at so young an age and in so short a time, and
several of his other writings have also been picked up
for English translation.

Among these minor works are lectures given at the
Evangelical Academy in Tutzing, Germany, on the
historical Jesus in 1960 (with his "doctor father,"
Günther Bornkamm), and on the origins of the
church (with Eduard Schweizer and another New
Testament scholar, August Strobel) in 1966. (For
titles and details, see the section entitled "For Further
Reading" at the close of this book.) Among his articles
in German periodicals and festschrifts are one on Old
Testament themes in early Christian traditions about
the Lord's Supper (I recall serving as impromptu
translator for a version of this paper read at a Society
for New Testament Studies seminar at Cambridge,
England, in 1966) and another on "scripture and tradition" in primitive Christianity (relevant to what
he has to say in this book in the section in Chapter

VIII on the public reading of scripture), both printed in the periodical *Evangelische Theologie*. Professor Hahn has been editor for the Meyer commentary series (Kritisch-exegetischer Kommentar) since 1971, and currently is a coeditor for the series Biblische Studien and WMANT (Neukirchener Verlag) and the journal *Verkündigung und Forschung*. It might be added that Wilhelm Hahn, mentioned in the notes of this book as the author of a standard study on worship, is not related.

Certain characteristics of Ferdinand Hahn's work as a whole run through the essay before us on worship. The first has to do with his tendency to survey the whole sweep of a topic in the New Testament and to see it panoramically from an overall historical perspective. Thus the book at hand takes up, in chapter after chapter, worship in ancient Israel and in Judaism at the time of Jesus; Jesus' ministry and attitudes; then worship in the developing church, stage by stage, in the New Testament period, down into subapostolic times, and finally in the Apostolic Fathers and beyond. (Actually some of the "Apostolic Fathers," like Clement of Rome, [ca. A.D. 95], the Didache or "Teaching of the Twelve Apostles" [ca. A.D. 100], and Ignatius of Antioch, are contemporary with or earlier than the last documents to be written in the New Testament.)

Such a survey was also announced in the study on the titles of Jesus ("Their History in Early Christianity," the subtitle says), though actually that book on "Son of man," "Lord," "Christ," "Son of David," "Son of God," and the notion of the "eschatological prophet" confined itself pretty much to the Gospel of Mark and the Synoptic tradition. In the book on mission such a scheme is better carried out: Old Testament and Jewish presuppositions, Jesus' attitude, and then early Christianity from the oldest layers of tradition down to the more recent ones. Thus, Hahn tends to treat whatever topic he tackles within the broad and developing stream of early Christian history. That gives perspective to his work on worship.

One particular feature of this tendency toward historical survey must be commented upon, however. That is the practice of analyzing early Christian history in terms of at least four stages in the New Testament period. First comes the original community (Urgemeinde) in Palestine. This group is assumed to have spoken the Aramaic language. Hence certain clues, from Aramaic idiom and vocabulary and Palestinian life, can be used to identify materials from this brief but basic period. Secondly, the gospel of Jesus soon spread among Jewish believers who spoke Greek rather than Aramaic (and such existed, even in Jerusalem) and among Jews of the Diaspora, scattered throughout the Greco-Roman world. Hellenistic Jewish Christianity represents an important second stage in development, short-lived but extremely significant as a bridge to the pagan world beyond Palestine.

Stage three is Gentile Christianity—pagans from the Greco-Roman world who come to faith in Jesus without ever having been Jews. Their language is Greek (though they retain a few Aramaic words in worship), their scriptures are in Greek (but they use the He-

brew Bible in one of its several existing translations),
and their way of thinking is often Greek (though in
service of the salvation which is "of the Jews"). Then
there is a fourth stage, what Hahn calls in the volume
on worship "the subapostolic period," from A.D. 60
or 70 to A.D. 100. Peter, Paul, and other early Christian contemporaries had careers which ran through
the first three stages and were in contact with the
earliest community, Hellenistic Jewish, and Gentile
Christianity; when they died who had been apostles
in any of the technical senses in which the term is
used in the New Testament, an era ended and subapostolic times began. Finally, since some New Testament documents like 2 Peter (perhaps as late as A.D.
150) fall into the second century, it is also possible to
count as a fifth stage within the period covered by the
New Testament the times when the Apostolic Fathers
and even the apologists (down to Justin Martyr) were
at work.

This penchant for analyzing the New Testament
in terms of historical stages of its development is a
characteristic of the Bultmann School. Hahn has
applied it faithfully in his other books. Note the
stages in his works on christological titles and mission: the Palestinian tradition or "the particularistic
Jewish Christianity of Palestine"; Hellenistic Jewish
Christianity; Gentile Christianity, etc. (these are
subdivisions in his chapters). Readers unfamiliar
with the method (and some who know it but object)
will raise questions at particularly two points: (1)
the paucity of source material for the first two stages;
(2) the multitude of documents which are lumped

together in the subapostolic period (Colossians, Ephesians, 1 Peter, James, the Pastoral Epistles, Hebrews, and Revelation, not to mention the Fourth Gospel and the Johannine Epistles)—indeed, most of the New Testament, save for Paul's genuine letters, is regarded as composed after A.D. 70. The answers are, as to point (1), that Hahn admits we must operate from indirect evidence for the early periods, but he makes use of sources and traditions embedded in our later documents; and as to point (2), that matters of authorship and date which are common critical conclusions—e.g., that Colossians and Ephesians are not by Paul; that 1 Peter is not by Cephas (Simon Peter); that our gospels were all written around A.D. 70–100—are to be accepted and their implications drawn.

That brings us to a second major characteristic in Hahn's work generally and in this book on worship in particular. In part it has already been implied. He employs the historical-critical method, as practiced in German scholarship, of the Bultmann School. His use of this method was apparent above with regard to authorship and dates of documents and with regard to the sifting of traditions to recover the various layers. Something of this is, of course, to be expected of all biblical studies today, and the only question is the degree of rigor with which it is applied. That such rigorous criticism has not always been applied in the study of early Christian worship is very true, and Hahn's methodology serves both to settle old debates and raise new questions in this area.

What needs to be called to the reader's attention on this score is the particular habit of Hahn to employ the "tradition-history method" of approach. That is, he assumes, in tracing a theme, that a particular story or saying or practice first was recounted orally, subject to all the rules which the form critics have worked out for analyzing oral tradition. Then that tradition probably got incorporated in some larger collection or was even written down in a document that served as a source for some still later writer. Further, that writer who preserves for us the earlier tradition or source no doubt had his own interests and concerns in the situation he was facing, and so, as he used and edited this source, he also functioned as a theologian (as I shall, a few paragraphs later in this Introduction, in citing Peter Brunner). Hence the skills of oral and source criticism and redaction history must be used to lay out the trajectory which a tradition followed. The object is to employ evidence from each ascertainable part of many such trajectories or reconstructions of a theme to learn what worship was like overall at the various stages of Christian development.

Again, those unaccustomed to the tradition-history approach may be nonplused at some of the applications and results. But two things must be said. (1) This method fruitfully allows the critic to say something about the twilight period prior to the time from which we have documents. Paul's epistles, especially 1 Corinthians, tell us bits about worship in the fifth decade of the first century. But what happened to the thirties and forties? There once was a type of scholarship that liked to fill in the blanks by inserting generous quantities of later beliefs and practices, even from the second century. That approach is ruled out by our awareness that many of these are later developments. The alternative had traditionally been to employ the opening chapters of the Acts of the Apostles to give us a picture of the earliest church. Now that Acts is recognized as a product of Luke and his theology for his day (though also employing earlier sources and traditions), we are aware that Acts "as is" will not suffice either. The critic thus welcomes the insights which indirect data afford regarding the Aramaic-speaking church and Hellenistic Jewish Christianity; indeed the evidence in Acts sometimes becomes more comprehensible in light of such illumination.

(2) Professor Hahn has often employed the tradition-history method more conservatively than radical practitioners of form criticism. A widely discussed example has to do with his handling of Peter's confession at Caesarea Philippi. Bultmann, in *The History of the Synoptic Tradition* (New York: Harper & Row, 1963), pp. 257–59, had regarded the whole story as a post-Easter creation of the early church, and it has become a commonplace to deny that the title "Christ" was ever used by, or even of, Jesus during his lifetime. Hahn, however, in his book on the titles of Jesus, reckons with the ways in which the term "messiah" (Christ) was used in Jesus' lifetime—mostly in a zealot manner, for a leader who might lead a revolt against Rome—and conjectures that, tradition-historically, behind Mark 8:27–33, stands a historical story where Peter offered a messianic confession of zealot mould (v. 29b), which

Jesus rejected (v. 33). In his book on mission Hahn finds evidence enough to write a chapter on "Jesus' Attitude to the Gentiles." Likewise in the study before us: tradition history yields findings on Jesus' views about the sabbath, fasting, laws concerning ritual purity, prayer, and the temple (Chapter III).

A third characteristic of this study on worship which also emerges in some of Professor Hahn's other work has to do with what might be called "theological stance." In tracing Hahn's career we have noted above his brief involvement in the ministry and his lecturing at academies for lay people and those outside academic and even church circles. When the Evangelical Church in Germany (EKD) was planning its synod for May, 1970, in Stuttgart, Professor Hahn was invited to give a major theological address to it on "Responsibility for the Gospel in the World." The aim, in part, was to balance with theological concern the intense practical discussions caused at that meeting by the withdrawal of the territorial churches in East Germany (Landeskirchen in the DDR, up to then part of EKD). Professor Hahn's lecture dealt with the very proprium of the church—what constitutes its essence—and what is its responsibility in the world. To balance his presentation and theses, in turn, a further response was appended by a systematician, Gerhard Sauter, one of the "theologians of hope," and the whole printed in the series Theologische Existenz heute. To cite a final example, readers of the essay before us will note one reference to a difficult New Testament passage on which Hahn has written a homiletical treatment in an exegetical series for German preachers (see Chapter VIII, n. 29).

The particular relevance for us here of this churchly involvement and theological stance has to do with the general attitude taken toward worship by Professor Hahn. He is, after all, a member of the Evangelical Church and teaches in an Evangelical faculty. In fairness, readers should be alerted to this as grounds for a possible "tendency," though remembering that Catholic colleagues thought well enough of his historical objectivity (and perhaps also any "theological stance"!) to have *Der urchristliche Gottesdienst* published in a Catholic series.

The German and specifically Evangelical background of the essay should be noted at one particular point, however, where also a celebrated problem of translation occurs. Hahn's German title, in both printed versions, was *Der urchristliche Gottesdienst,* which might, rather literally, be rendered, "The Primitive Christian Service of God." That same word "Gottesdienst" runs through most of his chapter titles (II–IX; der Gottesdienst, e.g., of the Aramaic-speaking community, of the subapostolic period, etc.). In conformity with usual practice in translation, "Gottesdienst" has regularly been rendered as "worship" below—*The Worship of the Early Church,* "Worship in the Old Testament and Judaism" (Chapter II), and so through Chapter IX. However, beneath this rendering a potential difference in outlook lurks which divides German Evangelical and English-language approaches.

"Worship" is a general term in English for

reverence, honor, or respect toward a person of great rank or a deity. Deriving from the Anglo-Saxon "worthship," it implies a quality within the object of worship which calls forth "worship." "His worth-ship calls for my worship." Hence, in dictionary definitions the verb regularly means "to venerate, adore, pay divine honors," and "perform religious acts of homage." The German "Gottesdienst" means "service of God," but the tricky question is whether to take the genitive, "Gottes-," "God's service," as an objective or subjective genitive. The former would make God the object of the action in serving; Gottes-dienst in this sense would be "serving God" and im-plies much of what "worship" does—honor, venera-tion, acts of homage, e.g., in cult. The subjective genitive, however, takes the "Gottes-" part of the compound·as the subject of the action of serving, and so the sense is "God's serving us." Worship, on that reading, means when God ministers to men and brings the Good News and his grace into their lives.

The Evangelical tradition, especially in Germany, has regularly understood Gottesdienst (worship) in this latter sense, as the Gospel note of God doing something for us which we cannot do for ourselves. It is obvious, from his conclusions in Chapter X, that Professor Hahn understands Gottesdienst (what we have rendered "worship") in precisely this sense: the basis of worship is God's saving action; word and sacraments are God's service to the community. Coupled with it is, however, also a reciprocal aspect, the response side from man, namely, service by the community before God. But as Professor Hahn reads the New Testament—and again this is characteristic of Evangelical thought, in light of Romans 12—the church's service before God takes place in the world and especially takes the form of service to the brother. The two aspects have been set forth by the Lutheran theologian at Heidelberg whom Hahn cites (Chapter X, n.1), Peter Brunner, in his study, *Worship* (Gottesdienst) *in the Name of Jesus:*

> worship as a service of God to the congregation;
> worship as the congregation's service before God.

Such an understanding of worship stands many conventional definitions on their heads. Its emphasis on service by the believing community in the world should speak to many today who urge the church in just such a direction, to such tasks. It is that understanding which the essay before us advocates. (From the standpoint of an Old Testament scholar, some of the same emphases appear in a 1953 essay by George Mendenhall, listed under "For Further Reading.")

There are a number of other striking features and emphases in Professor Hahn's presentation which the reader will want to weigh for himself: the missionary factor to worship, even to the sacraments; or the attempt to discern charismatic elements in early Christianity as well as those of more sober style which led to patristic norms (I regard the attempt to use the Gospel to mediate among these varieties of New Testament worship as a significant contribution). The book repudiates alternate approaches which would center worship in some later emphasis or start from some second-century vantage point, e.g., eucharist or ministry. It also distinguishes itself from presentations which isolate elements in early Christian worship and never give us an overall approach. Against Oscar Cullmann (but with Walter Bauer), he holds that not all early Christian worship was eucharistic. Against C. F. D. Moule, he places less emphasis on synagogue backgrounds (and even less on the temple, the alternative which Moule too played down) and more on Christian creativity. In contrast to Gerhard Delling (to mention one other writer on worship in the New Testament), he makes his subject more than a series of separate items. And in the old debate of Sohm against Harnack, over the Spirit and charismata vs. "church law," he tends to side with the former, or at least to take seriously the charismatic side. Gospel, freedom, Spirit; appreciation for varieties of early Christian experiences at worship; and the concept of Gottesdienst sketched above, mark Professor Hahn's survey.

The translation has been made from the 1970 revised German version. It is the work of David E. Green, Librarian at San Francisco Theological Seminary and the Graduate Theological Union, Berkeley, who is known for his translation of works in the biblical field. He has also provided most of the detailed bibliographical data on German titles mentioned by Professor Hahn and, where they exist, their English equivalents. The bibliography of books on worship at the end is that provided by the author himself. Occasionally in the footnotes, especially where the major reference was to a title in German, recent literature in English has been added by the editor. Granted, the titles in the footnotes take up a good portion of the book, but the author, along with posing the problems and giving his own views, has as an aim to "survey . . . the relevant literature." We have not, however, in the footnotes, repeated details on a German work where there is a translation; for that, the original essays of Hahn can be consulted. Renderings of New Testament passages sometimes follow the RSV, other times they are original. Technical terms, like "homology" (Greek *homologia,* confession) and "parenesis" (Greek *parainesis,* ethical exhortation), which are now common in biblical studies have been retained where the author has them. The temptation to add further bibliography on many of the topics discussed has been resisted; titles under "For Further Reading" will provide such references.

JOHN REUMANN
Lutheran Theological Seminary, Philadelphia
August 4, 1972

Author's Preface

The present study of early Christian worship was written in 1966 at the request of Dr. Karl Ferdinand Müller, director of the Kirchenmusikschule Hannover, for the *Jahrbuch für Liturgik und Hymnologie,* which he edits. It appeared in Volume 12 (1967), pp. 1–44. I was happy to accept the suggestion of Professor Wilhelm Pesch, my colleague at Mainz, to republish my findings in the Stuttgarter Bibelstudien series. I am most grateful to him and the other editors of the series for their willingness to accept the work of a Protestant scholar. It is a good sign of the ecumenical cooperation that has become possible, and suggests how our churches share common problems.

It was the purpose of my study to survey as concisely as possible the problems and the relevant literature, and outline my own view of the matter. This purpose has not been changed for the present publication, which differs from the initial publication only in the correction of certain details and the addition of considerable additional bibliography.

Hochheim/Main, August 2, 1969

Abbreviations

AGSU	Arbeiten zur Geschichte des Spätjudentums und Urchristentums (Leiden: Brill)
AnBib	Analecta Biblica (Rome: Pontifical Biblical Institute)
ASNU	Acta Seminarii Neotestamentici Upsaliensis (Uppsala: Gleerup; Copenhagen: Munksgard)
ATANT	Abhandlungen zur Theologie des Alten und Neuen Testaments (Zurich:Zwingli)
BEvT	Beiträge zur evangelischen Theologie (Munich: Kaiser)
BFChrTh	Beiträge zur Förderung christlicher Theologie (Gütersloh: Bertelsmann)
BWANT	Beiträge zur Wissenschaft vom Alten und Neuen Testament (Stuttgart: Kohlhammer)
BZ	*Biblische Zeitschrift*
BZAW	Beihefte zur Zeitschrift für die alttestamentliche Wissenschaft (Berlin: Töpelmann)
BZNW	Beihefte zur Zeitschrift für die neutestamentliche Wissenschaft (Berlin: Töpelmann)
ESW	Ecumenical Studies in Worship (London: Lutterworth; Richmond: John Knox)
EvT	*Evangelische Theologie*
FBBS	Facet Books Biblical Series (Philadelphia: Fortress)

FRLANT Forschungen zur Religion und Literatur des Alten und Neuen Testaments (Göttingen: Vandenhoeck & Ruprecht)

HNT Handbuch zum Neuen Testament (Tübingen: Mohr)

HTKNT Herders theologischer Kommentar zum Neuen Testament (Freiburg: Herder)

JLH *Jahrbuch für Liturgik und Hymnologie* (Kassel)

KEK Kritisch-Exegetischer Kommentar über das Neue Testament, begründet von H. A. W. Meyer (Göttingen: Vandenhoeck & Ruprecht)

NF Neue Folge

NovT *Novum Testamentum*

NTA Neutestamentliche Abhandlungen (Gütersloh: Bertelsmann; later, and NF, Münster: Aschendorff)

NTAbstracts *New Testament Abstracts*

NTS *New Testament Studies*

RGG *Die Religion in Geschichte und Gegenwart*, 3d ed., ed. K. Galling et al., 7 vols. (Tübingen: Mohr, 1957–65)

SBib Stuttgarter Bibelstudien (Stuttgart: Katholisches Bibelwerk)

SBT Studies in Biblical Theology (London: SCM; Chicago: Henry Regnery, later Naperville: Alec R. Allenson; cited by volume number; second series thus: 2/1)

SNTSMS Society for New Testament Studies Monograph Series (New York: Cambridge University Press)

StANT Studien zum Alten und Neuen Testament (Munich: Kösel)

TDNT *Theological Dictionary of the New Testament*, ed. Gerhard Kittel and Gerhard

	Friedrich, trans. of *ThW* by G. W. Bromiley, in process (Grand Rapids: Eerdmans, 1964– ; Vol. 1 [1964]; 2 [1964]; 3 [1965]; 4 [1967]; 5 [1967]; 6[1968]; 7 [1971]; 8 [1972])
ThBl	*Theologische Blätter*
ThBü	Theologische Bücherei (Munich: Kaiser)
THK	Theologischer Handkommentar zum Neuen Testament (Berlin: Evangelische Verlagsanstalt)
ThR	*Theologische Rundschau*
ThW	*Theologisches Wörterbuch zum Neuen Testament,* ed. G. Kittel and G. Friedrich, 10 vols. (Stuttgart: Kohlhammer, 1933– ; cited in its Eng. trans. *TDNT* where available as of 1972)
TLZ	*Theologische Literaturzeitung*
TU	Texte und Untersuchungen (Berlin: Akademie Verlag)
TZ	*Theologische Zeitschrift*
VC	*Vigiliae Christianae*
WMANT	Wissenschaftliche Monographien zum Alten und Neuen Testament (Neukirchen-Vluyn: Neukirchener Verlag)
ZNW	*Zeitschrift für die neutestamentliche Wissenschaft*
ZTK	*Zeitschrift für Theologie und Kirche*

The Bibliography at the end of this book ("For Further Reading") is only a partial one. Hence full information on titles cited in the book is given in the footnote the first time a title occurs. Thereafter, short titles are used in the notes, with a cross reference back to the first note where the full publication data were provided. Unless in such a cross reference the footnote number (n.) is preceded by a chapter designation, it refers to the note in the same chapter; thus:

"(cited above, n. 2)" refers to footnote 2 in the same chapter;

"(cited above, Chap. I, n. 2)" refers to a previous chapter. For series of monographs listed above, place and publisher are not repeated in the notes.

The Problem

It is a well-known fact that the earliest evidences from which we can derive a complete picture of the structure and sequence of Christian worship date from the middle of the second century.[1] All the records that have been preserved from the earlier period are extremely fragmentary. Not only are the sources incomplete, there is not even a consistent framework. The study of worship in the period of primitive Christianity therefore confronts numerous difficulties, some of them serious; methodological considerations alone suggest that texts from the first century and the first half of the second receive special treatment.[2]

1. For basic orientation, we cite only Hans Lietzmann, *Die Entstehung der christlichen Liturgie nach den ältesten Quellen*, Vorträge der Bibliothek Warburg, 5 (1925–26); reprinted, Libelli, 100 (Darmstadt: Wissenschaftliche Buchgesellschaft, 1963), and in his *Kleine Schriften*, ed. Kurt Aland, 3 vols., TU 67, 68, 74 (Berlin: Akademie Verlag, 1958–62), Vol. 3 (TU 74 [1962]), pp. 3–27; idem, "Der altchristliche Gottesdienst," in his *Kleine Schriften*, Vol. 3 (1962), pp. 28–42; William Nagel, *Geschichte des christlichen Gottesdienstes*, Sammlung Göschen, 1202/2a (Berlin: de Gruyter, 1962; 2d ed., 1970).

2. See in particular Johannes Leipoldt, *Der Gottesdienst der ältesten Kirche* (Leipzig: Dörffling & Franke, 1937): Josef Maria Nielen, *The Earliest Christian Liturgy*, trans. P. Cummins (St. Louis: Herder, 1941) Oscar Cullmann, *Early Christian Worship*, trans. A. S. Todd and J. B. Torrance, SBT 10 (1953); 2d ed., 1962) ; Wilhelm T. Hahn, *Gottesdienst und Opfer Christi* (Berlin: Evangelische Verlagsanstalt, 1951); Gerhard Delling, *Worship in the New Testament*, trans. Percy Scott (Philadelphia; Westminster, 1962) ; C. F. D. Moule, *Worship in the New Testament*, ESW 9 (1961);

In the New Testament we find a wealth of individual elements deriving from the worship of the primitive church. Some appear with a certain regularity,
but in most cases it is extremely difficult to make out
any relationship between them. There is no trace of
any obligatory liturgical order. We must instead think
in terms of great freedom and variety in the structur-
ing of worship. It is therefore all the more necessary
to inquire into the common intention of early Christian worship, its nature and its uniqueness. Under no
circumstances is it sufficient to limit a study of the
New Testament data to the individual elements.[3]
This approach will not succeed in comprehending the
uniqueness of early Christian worship. On the other
hand, one must not be too quick to take a specific
theological conception of the New Testament, for instance Paul's image of the body of Christ or the doctrine of Christ's high-priesthood found in Hebrews,
and make it the organizing principle of one's presentation.[4] The presuppositions must be elucidated in
each case; the particular controlling eschatological,
christological, and ecclesiological motifs must be
taken into account. Not only the variety of forms and
modes of expression, but also the variety of theological conceptions underlying each writer's understand-

and Ralph P. Martin, *Worship in the Early Church* (London:
Marshall, Morgan & Scott, 1964).

3. This stricture applies to a whole series of presentations of liturgical history. Even Delling's book (cited above, n. 2), despite its
important introductory and concluding sections, concentrates its
interest somewhat too much on the individual elements.

4. The presentations of Nielen and W. Hahn (cited above, n. 2)
are especially problematic in this respect. Nielen's book nevertheless offers a series of valuable studies of particular details. For a
discussion of W. Hahn, see below, pp. 105–7.

ing of worship, must be considered. Only then can we turn to the question of whether certain points of reference and common structures can be identified in the earliest period.

If it is to do justice to this task, a presentation must be organized so as to follow the history of primitive Christianity.[5] The New Testament provides evidence from various periods and geographical regions; even if it is not always possible to provide a detailed arrangement and precise tradition-historical classification of the individual traditions, it is possible to group them according to the major periods of early Christian history. We begin with a brief survey of worship in the Old Testament and Judaism, because the question of shared elements and dependence crops up repeatedly.[6] The next important point is the attitude of Jesus toward the worship of his period. Only a recognition of the motivation and impact of his conduct can explain how the primitive community, on the basis of the Easter and Pentecost event, could arrive at their own particular ordering of worship.[7] In the subsequent course of our study we must

5. Up to now, the only attempt along this line has been that of Leipoldt, *Gottesdienst* (cited above, n. 2). Compare the antithesis between sections 5–7 and 22 that is still found in Leonhard Goppelt, *Apostolic and Post-Apostolic Times,* trans. R. A. Guelich (New York: Harper & Row, 1970).

6. For discussions of this question, see especially W. O. E. Oesterley, *The Jewish Background of the Christian Liturgy* (Oxford: Clarendon, 1925); C. W. Dugmore, *The Influence of the Synagogue upon the Divine Office* (London: Oxford, 1944; reprinted Westminster: Faith Press, 1964); O. S. Rankin, "The Extent of the Influence of the Synagogue Service upon Christian Worship," *Journal of Jewish Studies* 1 (1948): pp. 27 ff.

7. This problem has been recognized and stated most clearly by Ernst Lohmeyer, *Lord of the Temple,* trans. S. Todd (Edinburgh:

distinguish the Aramaic-speaking Jewish Christianity
of Palestine from the community of Hellenistic Jewish Christians, which began to form very early.
Through the mediation of Hellenistic Jewish Christianity and its missionary activity there then sprang
up a Gentile Christian community and an independent Gentile Christian tradition. In the course of the
subapostolic period, from the sixties of the first century on, the various strands of tradition became
interwoven in different ways. This period paved the
way for the development in the second century that
within a relatively brief period led to a fixed liturgical
order.

The following presentation of the problems surrounding the worship of the early church ignores
many subsidiary questions. We must forgo any discussion of the formation of creeds, as well as baptism
and the Lord's Supper, and ecclesiastical office. The
complexity of these individual themes requires independent treatment for each. The questions associated
with these topics are touched on here only to the
extent that they bear on early Christian worship as a
whole. This may be surprising especially with regard
to the Lord's Supper; but it would be inappropriate
to approach the earliest history of Christian worship
solely from the perspective of how the eucharist developed.[8] This is not to dispute the great importance

Oliver & Boyd, 1961), but his perverse approach to the question
distorts the problem strangely.

8. Even so significant a work as Josef A. Jungmann's monumental
The Mass of the Roman Rite, 2 vols., trans. F. A. Brunnen (New
York; Benziger, 1951–55), Vol. 1, pp. 7 ff. (2d ed., rev. and abridged,

of the Lord's Supper; but our first task is to examine the liturgical life of the earliest community in its full breadth.

1959, pp. 3 ff.), is totally one-sided, taking as its point of departure the Last Supper and its evolution into the eucharist. Jungmann gives only cursory treatment to the influence of synagogue worship on the liturgy of the word in the proanaphora.

II

Worship in the
Old Testament and Judaism

Jewish worship at the time of Jesus must be understood as the product of a long history. In recent
decades, the history of the Israelite cult has been the
object of active investigation, which has clearly revealed the particulars of worship in the preexilic and
postexilic eras.[1] Its further development in the period
after the Old Testament has also been explained in
its essentials.[2] It is therefore not necessary to describe

1. Study of the Israelite cult received its primary initial impetus
from Julius Wellhausen, and has been significantly furthered by
Hermann Gunkel, Sigmund Mowinckel, Albrecht Alt, Gerhard von
Rad, and others. See the comprehensive presentation in Hans-
Joachim Kraus, *Worship in Israel*, trans. G. Buswell from the 2d
German ed. (Richmond: John Knox, 1966; the 1st German ed. in
1954 comprised only studies devoted to the Feast of Booths). See
also R. Rendtorff, "Der Kultus im alten Israel," *JLH* 2 (1956):
1–21 (treating only the preexilic period); A. S. Herbert, *Worship
in Ancient Israel*, ESW 5 (1959); H. H. Rowley, *Worship in Israel*,
Edward Cadbury Lectures, 1966 (London: SPCK, 1967).

2. See the studies of Emil Schürer, *History of the Jewish People in
the Time of Jesus Christ*, trans. John Macpherson et al., 5 vols.,
Clark's Foreign Theological Library, New Series, 23–25, 41, 43
(Edinburgh: T. & T. Clark, 1885–1902), Vols. 23, 24 (=Division II,
Vols. 1, 2), sections 22 ff., especially 24, 27, 28; H. L. Strack & P.
Billerbeck, *Kommentar zum Neuen Testament aus Talmud und
Midrasch*, 6 vols. in 7 (Munich: Beck, 1922–28, reprinted in 6 vols.
1965–69), Vol. 4/1 (1928), Excurses 4–12; I. Elbogen, *Der jüdische
Gottesdienst in seiner geschichtlichen Entwicklung*, Grundriss der
Gesamtwissenschaft des Judentums (Leipzig: Fock, 1913; 3d ed.,
Frankfurt: Kauffmann, 1931; reprinted as 4th ed., Hildesheim:
Olms, 1962), especially pp. 232 ff.; idem (with E. Lohse), "Gottes-
dienst, III. Synagogaler," in *RGG*, Vol. 2, cols. 1756–61; W. Schrage,
"synagōgē," in *TDNT*, Vol. 7, pp. 798–852.

in detail the origin and development of worship down to the time of Jesus; we can restrict ourselves to noting the major phases.

There were two preliminary components that produced specifically Israelite worship: worship of the "God of the fathers" on the part of the desert tribes;[3] and the Yahweh cult of the early period, associated with the Sinai tradition. Worship of the "God of the fathers" probably included the pre-Yahwistic original form of Passover.[4] In the earliest Yahweh cult,[5] the tabernacle tradition played an important role; the origin of the ark cult [6] and occurrence of the cove-

3. See A. Alt, "The God of the Fathers" in his *Essays on Old Testament History and Religion*, trans. R. A. Wilson (Oxford: Blackwell, 1966; Garden City: Doubleday Anchor Books, 1968), pp. 1–100; F. M. Cross, Jr., "Yahwe and the God of the Patriarchs," *Harvard Theological Review* 55 (1962) : 225–59; K. T. Andersen, "Der Gott meines Vaters," *Studia Theologica* 16 (Lund, 1962): 170–88; M. Haran, "The Religion of the Patriarchs," *Annual of the Swedish Theological Institute* 4 (Leiden: Brill, 1965): 30–55.

4. L. Rost, "Weidewechsel und alttestamentlicher Festkalender," *Zeitschrift des Deutschen Palästina-Vereins* 56 (1943): 205 ff., reprinted in his *Das kleine Credo und andere Studien zum Alten Testament* (Heidelberg: Quelle & Meyer, 1965), pp. 101–12; see also Kraus, *Worship in Israel* (cited above, n. 1), pp. 45 ff.; E. Kutsch, "Erwägungen zur Geschichte der Passafeier und des Massotfestes," *ZTK* 55 (1958): 1–35; J. B. Segal, *The Hebrew Passover*, London Oriental Series 12 (London: Oxford, 1963). Circumcision also goes back to the pre-Yahwistic period; see R. Meyer, "*peritemnō*," in *TDNT*, Vol. 6, pp. 72–84. The origin and age of the sabbath remain shrouded in uncertainty; see J. J. Stamm, "Dreissig Jahre Dekalogforschung," *ThR* NF 27 (1961): 189–239, 281–305, especially 290 ff.; J. J. Stamm and M. E. Andrew, *The Ten Commandments in Recent Research*, SBT 2/2 (1962), pp. 90–95.

5. See Rendtorff, "Kultus" (cited above, n. 1), pp. 4 ff.; G. von Rad, *Old Testament Theology*, trans. D. M. G. Stalker, 2 vols. (New York: Harper & Row, 1962–65), Vol. 1, pp. 15 ff., 129 ff.; Walter Beyerlin, *Origins and History of the Oldest Sinaitic Traditions*, trans. S. Rudman (Oxford: Blackwell, 1961), pp. 145 ff.; W. H. Schmidt, *Alttestamentlicher Glaube und seine Umwelt* (Neukirchen-Vluyn: Neukirchener Verlag, 1968), pp. 38 ff.

6. G. von Rad, "The Tent and the Ark," in his *The Problem of the Hexateuch and Other Essays*, trans. E. W. Trueman Dicken (New

nant concept [7] in the period before the occupation are disputed. Only after the entrance into Canaan was there a closer alliance, with the constitution of an Israelite amphictyony at the "Shechem assembly" (Joshua 24).[8] This establishment of a unity that was primarily sacral, not political, laid the groundwork for a specifically Israelite worship. For this early period, we unfortunately have little information about its nature and individual ceremonies.

Even in the early amphictyonic period certain traditions of the settled territory became associated with the faith of the Israelites; immediately afterward there was an extensive adoption of formerly Canaanite cultic practices and traditions.[9] A new stage was marked by the association of the amphictyonic cult with the Jebusite cult traditions of Jerusalem under

York: McGraw-Hill, 1966), pp. 103–24; Johann Maier, *Das altisraelitische Ladeheiligtum*, BZAW 93 (1965).

7. For the most recent discussion, see Dennis J. McCarthy, *Der Gottesbund im Alten Testament*, SBib 13 (1966), an expansion of his article, "Covenant in the Old Testament: the Present State of the Inquiry," in *Catholic Biblical Quarterly* 27 (1965): 217–40; expanded English version, *Old Testament Covenant: A Survey of Current Opinions* (Oxford: Basil Blackwell, 1972). E. Kutsch, "Von bᵉrît zu 'Bund'," *Kerygma und Dogma* 14 (1968): 159–82; R. Martin-Achard, "La signification de l'alliance dans l'Ancien Testament," *Revue de théologie et de philosophie* 101 (1968): 88–102; L. Perlitt, *Bundestheologie im Alten Testament*, WMANT 36 (1970).

8. Martin Noth, *Das System der zwölf Stämme Israels*, BWANT 4/1 (1930; reprinted Darmstadt: Wissenschaftliche Buchgesellschaft, 1966); also Rudolf Smend, *Yahweh War & Tribal Confederation*, trans. M. G. Rogers (Nashville: Abingdon, 1970), see pp. 76 ff. and 128 ff. for a discussion of the ark tradition; for a discussion of Joshua 24, see Götz Schmitt, *Der Landtag zu Sichem*, Arbeiten zur Theologie, 1/15 (Stuttgart: Calwer, 1964).

9. We may think primarily in terms of the adoption of Canaanite sanctuaries, as well as the great agricultural festivals, together with their incorporation into the religious traditions of Israel; see Rendtorff, "Kultus" (cited above, n. 1), pp. 13 ff.; von Rad, *Theology* (cited above, n. 5), Vol. 1, pp. 19 ff.

David, whereby Zion and the elect royal house, and finally also the temple built by Solomon, achieved special significance.[10]

The next decisive step was Josiah's centralization of the cult shortly before the exile,[11] which was based on Deuteronomic ideals. But when the temple was rebuilt in the postexilic period, the principles of the Priestly Document prevailed, which depended in turn on Ezekiel and the Holiness Code. The entire sacrificial and festival cult was associated with an all-encompassing propitiatory ritual, reaching its high point in the annual observance of the great Day of Atonement (Leviticus 16). This form of temple worship remained authoritative for the future.[12]

In this later period, the relationship of the synagogues to the temple and its cult took on great significance. The centralization of the cult, which had begun before the exile, gradually made the establishment of such houses for study necessary. The date of

10. See M. Noth, "Jerusalem und die israelitische Tradition," *Oudtestamentische Studien* 8 (1950): 28–46, reprinted in his *Gesammelte Studien zum Alten Testament*, ThBü 6, 39 (1957–69), Vol. 1 (2d. ed., 1960), pp. 172–87; idem, "Gott, König, Volk im Alten Testament," *ZTK* 47 (1950); 157–91, reprinted in *Gesammelte Studien*, Vol. 1, pp. 188–239; Kraus, *Worship in Israel* (cited above, n. 1), pp. 179 ff.; Joseph Schreiner, *Sion-Jerusalem, Jahwes Königssitz*, StANT 7 (1963).

11. See Martin Noth, *The History of Israel*, trans. S. Godman, 2d ed. rev. by P. R. Ackroyd (New York: Harper, 1960), pp. 269 ff.; E. W. Nicholson, "Josiah's Reformation and Deuteronomy," *Glasgow University Oriental Society Translations* 20 (1964): 77–84.

12. See K. Koch, "Die Eigenart der priesterschriftlichen Sinai-Gesetzgebung," *ZTK* 55 (1958): 36–51; von Rad, *Theology* (cited above, n. 5), Vol. 1, pp. 232 ff.; P. Billerbeck, "Ein Tempelgottesdienst in Jesu Tagen," *ZNW* 55 (1964): 1–17; Roland de Vaux, *Studies in Old Testament Sacrifice* (Cardiff: University of Wales Press, 1964); R. Rendtorff, *Studien zur Geschichte des Opfers im Alten Israel*, WMANT 24 (1967).

the first synagogues has long been a matter of debate; the first firm evidence dates from the third century B.C.[13] They served primarily for liturgical assembly on the sabbath, in the course of which the law was read, the people confessed the one God, and prayers were recited together.[14]

Through the synagogues, the Pharisees and scribes[15] gained enormous influence over the people. They cultivated a strict ritualism like that expressed in the sabbath regulations and the laws governing ritual purity.[16] We are dealing here with an attempt to order all of life in relationship to the temple cult from a sacral perspective and to give cultic ideology an unlimited priority.[17] Of course one must not overlook the fact that before A.D. 70 Judaism did not yet bear the exclusive stamp of Pharisaism. Besides the so-called *'am hā'āres* or "people of the land" (the poorer classes who did not know the intricacies of the law), there were various dissimilar religious groups: the priestly Sadducees,[18] the likewise priestly Qumran

13. See Schrage, *"synagōgē," TDNT*, Vol. 7, pp. 810 ff.

14. Besides the literature mentioned in n. 2 above, see P. Billerbeck, "Ein Synagogengottesdienst in Jesu Tagen," *ZNW* 55 (1964): 143–61.

15. Mark 2:16 ("the scribes of the Pharisees") demonstrates clearly that there were scribes not only among the Pharisees, but also among the Sadducees, etc. But the Pharisaic scribes played the crucial role, and are the ones referred to throughout the New Testament. See J. Wellhausen, *Pharisäer und Sadduzäer* (Greifswald Bamberg, 1874; 3d ed., Göttingen: Vandenhoeck & Ruprecht, 1967); T. Herford, *The Pharisees* (New York: Macmillan, 1924; reprinted Boston: Beacon, 1962); R. Meyer and H. F. Weiss, *"Pharisaios,"* in *ThW*, Vol. 9 (1969) , pp. 11–51.

16. See E. Lohse, *"sabbaton,"* in *TDNT*, Vol. 7, pp. 1–35; R. Meyer, *"katharos* (Judentum)," in *TDNT*, Vol. 3, pp. 418–23.

17. This applies primarily to the territory of Palestine. Unfortunately we know few details about the synagogue and Pharisaism in the Diaspora.

18. R Meyer, *"Saddoukaioi,"* in *TDNT*, Vol. 7, pp. 35–54.

community,[19] apocalyptic circles,[20] and the Zealots.[21] But the Sadducees exercised little influence, the Qumran community had gone its own separate way and established a monastic settlement in the desert, the apocalyptic circles obviously lived a withdrawn life, and the Zealots resembled the Pharisees in many ways. So it is not accidental that Jesus' crucial conflict was with the religious practice of the Pharisees.[22]

19. For orientation, see K. G. Kuhn, "Qumran," in *RGG*, Vol. 4, cols. 745–54; F. M. Cross, Jr., *The Ancient Library of Qumrân and Modern Biblical Studies*, Haskell Lectures, 1956–57 (Garden City: Doubleday, 1958; 2d ed., 1961); H. Bardtke, "Qumran und seine Probleme," *ThR* 33 (1968): 97–119, 185–236.

20. Unfortunately we have no clear data concerning the representatives of the apocalyptic tradition. This whole complex of problems deserves a new examination. See R. H. Charles, *Religious Development Between the Old and the New Testament* (New York: Holt, 1914); idem, "Eschatology," in *Encyclopaedia Britannica*, 10th ed. (1901); idem, *The Doctrine of a Future Life in Israel, in Judaism, and in Christianity—A Critical History* (1899; 2d ed., 1913), reprinted as *Eschatology* . . . , Introduction by G. W. Buchanan (New York: Schocken Books, 1963); W. Bousset and H. Gressmann, *Die Religion des Judentums im späthellenistischen Zeitalter*, HNT 21 (3d ed., 1926, reprinted as 4th ed., 1966), pp. 206 ff.; P. Volz, *Die Eschatologie der jüdischen Gemeinde im neutestamentlichen Zeitalter* (Tübingen: Mohr, 1934; reprinted Hildesheim: Olms, 1966); H. H. Rowley, *The Relevance of Apocalyptic* (London: Lutterworth, 1944; 3d ed., 1963); D. S. Russell, *The Method and Message of Jewish Apocalyptic* (Philadelphia: Westminster, 1964); for a history of studies in this area, see J. M. Schmidt, *Die jüdische Apokalyptik* (Neukirchen-Vluyn: Neukirchener Verlag, 1969).

21. M. Hengel, *Die Zeloten*, AGSU 1 (1965).

22. In the Gospels, above all in Matthew, we find a tendency to look upon the Pharisees as the sole representatives of Judaism, in accordance with the situation after A.D. 70; see Reinhard Hummel, *Die Auseinandersetzung zwischen Judentum und Christentum im Matthäusevangelium*, BEvT 33, 2d ed. (1966). The Gospel of John speaks only in general terms of the "Jews," but has in mind thereby the Pharisees especially. See L. Goppelt, *Christentum und Judentum im ersten und zweiten Jahrhundert*, BFChrTh 2/55 (1954), pp. 251 ff.; E. Grässer, "Die antijüdische Polemik im Johannesevangelium," *NTS* 11 (1964/65): 74–90, especially p. 77, n. 10; W. G. Kümmel, "Die Weherufe über die Schriftgelehrten und Pharisäer (Matthäus 23, 13–36)," in W. P. Eckert, N. P. Levinson, and M. Stöhr (eds.), *Antijudaismus im Neuen Testament?* (Munich: Kaiser, 1967), pp. 135–47.

III

Jesus' Attitude
toward Worship

When we turn to the ministry of Jesus and inquire about his attitude toward Jewish worship, we can agree with J. M. Nielen: our first impression is "indisputably one of a contradictory approach combining both freedom and constraint, impossible to harmonize into a single whole."[1] But careful study must determine just where we must speak of constraint, and what significance attaches to the freedom Jesus claimed for himself. He is undoubtedly constrained by the confession of the one God: "Hear, O Israel, the Lord our God is *one* God";[2] he is constrained by the necessity of witnessing to the operation of this

1. Nielen, *Liturgy* (cited above, Chap. I, n. 2), p. 55 (trans. above by David E. Green, to fit Hahn's development of the terms "Gebundenheit" and "Freiheit"). In any case it is improper to eliminate the tension between constraint and freedom by reducing them to a common denominator of inward disposition and outward ceremonial, as Nielen does on pp. 70 ff., especially 76–78.

2. Mark 12:29; we are dealing here with Deut. 6:4, the beginning of the so-called Shema, which had already claimed an important place in the liturgical practice of contemporary Judaism. See Elbogen, *Gottesdienst* (cited above, Chap. II, n. 2), pp. 16 ff.; Billerbeck (cited above, Chap. II, n. 2), Vol. 4/1, pp. 189 ff.; K. G. Kuhn, *Phylakterien aus Höhle 4 von Qumran*, Abhandlungen der Heidelberger Akademie der Wissenschaft, Phil.-Hist. Klasse, 1957, Abh. 1 (Heidelberg: Winter, 1957). Even if the citation of Deut. 6:4 in Mark 12:29 does not go back directly to Jesus (the Shema is missing in the two parallels Matt. 22:37 and Luke 10:27), his adherence to the fundamental creed of Israel is unmistakable.

God in creation and revelation.[3] He is likewise constrained by the original will of God; but for him the
constraint imposed by what God wills and requires
does not mean that he is bound by the Old Testament
law, much less the various traditions of pious Jews.[4]
What is crucial for Jesus is not what God has done
and required in the past, but his eschatological action
in the present. He therefore proclaimed the irruption of God's eschatological rule.[5] The eschatological
novelty of this message also explains its impact on the
old order; this is the basis of Jesus' freedom with respect to the totality of Old Testament and Jewish
tradition. In the metaphors of the new patch and
the new wine (Mark 2:21–22) there is no question
of any continuity between the old and the new: the
old existing order is not supplemented, renovated, or
continued; it must shatter, because what is permanent

3. See, for example, Matt. 5:45 and the discussion in G. Bornkamm,
Jesus of Nazareth, trans. Irene and Fraser McLuskey with James
M. Robinson (New York: Harper, 1960), pp. 117 ff.
4. See on the one hand Matt. 5:21–48; Mark 10:1–9, and on the
other Mark 7:1–8, with parallels. Under no circumstances, however,
is it correct to understand Jesus' attitude as Sadducaic adherence to
the law, discarding interpretive tradition. God's eschatological act
instead reveals God's primordial will in its still unbroken state. An
identification of the eschaton (Endzeit) and the primordial age
(Urzeit) may be operative here, giving rise to criticism of the law.
5. Although we are dealing with a revelation of God's salvation
that has power to overcome the world in the sense of apocalyptic
expectations, the traditional apocalyptic conception with its schema
of two aeons has been totally abandoned; for the kingship of God
is already being realized in the midst of the transitory world.
There is no space here to discuss the individual problems surround-
ing Jesus' proclamation of the kingdom or kingship of God; see
Bornkamm, *Jesus* (cited above, n. 3), pp. 64 ff.; H. Conzelmann,
"Reich Gottes," in *RGG*, Vol. 5, cols. 914–18; Rudolf Schnackenburg,
God's Rule and Kingdom, trans. John Murray (New York: Herder
& Herder, 1963); Eberhard Jüngel, *Paulus und Jesus* (Tübingen:
Mohr, 3d ed., 1967), pp. 71 ff.; Helmut Flender, *Die Botschaft
Jesu von der Herrschaft Gottes* (Munich: Kaiser, 1968).

and final is revealed. This does not imply a dualistic antithesis; the new is based in all respects on the old. But what is now disclosed is God's crucial action and undiminished will coming into play; it is a fulfillment that bursts and transcends all promises.[6]

This perspective makes it easier to understand Jesus' attitude toward Jewish worship. When he visits synagogue and temple, he goes primarily to proclaim his message and to act. Even more important, he does not limit his teaching and activity to the place of worship. Of course the Pharisees and scribes, too, exercised a public ministry; but such a ministry takes on special significance in the case of Jesus, because his proclamation cannot be fitted into the existing order and is associated with radical criticism of traditional worship.

This can already be seen when Jesus acts on his own authority on the sabbath, a trait recorded in a relatively large number of pericopes. Ever since the exile, this day of rest and worship had been strictly observed [7] as a means of distinguishing the Jews sharply from any Gentile way of life. On the sabbath Jesus did or permitted things that, according to the

6. Thus one can say that Jesus came to fulfill the law and the prophets (Matt. 5:17); but this statement must not be interpreted in the Jewish-Christian sense that not a letter or dot of the law can pass away (Matt. 5:18). On the problems posed by Matt. 5:17–20, see W. Trilling, *Das wahre Israel* (originally Leipzig: St. Benno, 1959; 3d ed., StANT 10 [1964]), pp. 165 ff.; G. Harder, "Jesus und das Gesetz (Matthäus 5, 17–20)," in Eckert, *Antijudaismus* (cited above, Chap. II, n. 22), pp. 105–18.

7. See Ernst Jenni, *Die theologische Begründung des Sabbatgebots im Alten Testament*, Theologische Studien 46 (Zollikon-Zurich: Evangelischer Verlag, 1956); Willy Rordorf, *Sunday: The History of the Day of Rest and Worship in the Earliest Centuries of the Christian Church*, trans. A. A. K. Graham (Philadelphia: Westminster, 1968), pp. 10 ff., 45 ff.

view then current, affected not only religious tradition but the very law itself. On the occasion when his disciples are plucking grain (Mark 2:23–28 and parallels), Jesus refers to the example of David, casting doubt on the binding force of the sabbath commandment. He then goes on to say, "The sabbath was made for man, and not man for the sabbath" (v. 27). A scandalous statement to Jewish ears—but even early Christianity sought to make it less radical by appending the saying about the special authority of the Son of man (v. 28), with the result that the original statement of the Lord was eventually omitted entirely.[8] Jesus is concerned that the sabbath be understood as an expression of God's mercy and beneficence toward man; and so, in the face of law and tradition, he discloses God's true will through his eschatological act. The concrete significance of this will is shown above all by the healings on the sabbath;[9] their essence is revealed in the question Jesus puts to those who are trying to trap him: "Is it permitted to do good or to do evil on the sabbath, to save life or to kill?" (Mark 3:4). In principle the saving of life was not forbidden on the sabbath, but was absolutely allowed in cases of acute danger. Jesus, however, wants to have this principle put into practice without

8. Matthew and Luke omit it. For a discussion of the individual problems of the text, see Ernst Käsemann, "The Problem of the Historical Jesus" (1954), Eng. trans. W. J. Montague in Käsemann's *Essays on New Testament Themes*, SBT 41 (1964), pp. 15–47 (the relevant passage will be found on pp. 38 ff.) ; Rordorf, *Sunday* (cited above, n. 7), pp. 59 ff.

9. The primary traditions are Mark 3:1–6 and Luke 13:10–17; Luke 14:1–6 probably exhibits marked influence of or dependence on Mark 3:1–6; John 5:1–9a, 9b–13; 9:1–7 (8–12) 13 ff. were not originally sabbath narratives.

restrictions.[10] As a consequence, he breaks the traditional rules of the sabbath.

What holds for sabbath observance is applied in like fashion by Jesus to the regulations governing cleanness and uncleanness. These, too, had been legitimized by the law, albeit significantly extended in detail by tradition.[11] Jesus no more distinguished in principle between written torah and oral tradition than did his opponents.[12] Mark 7:1–23/Matt. 15:1–20, a text that presents tradition-historical difficulties and contains several strata, is instructive. The practice of corban rejected in Mark 7:9–13 refers to the temple cult. The first points of interest here are Mark 7:1a, 2, 5, together with Mark 7:6–8, dealing with ritual hand-washing, and the logion Mark 7:15.[13] According to v. 8, Jesus' crucial point is that the Pharisees and scribes do not even follow the true commandment of God, but adhere instead to ordinances of

10. Cf. the objection in Luke 13:14 and the statements of the Lord in Luke 13:15; 14:5.

11. See W. G. Kümmel, "Jesus und der jüdische Traditionsgedanke," *ZNW* 33 (1934): 105–30; reprinted in his *Heilsgeschehen und Geschichte: Gesammelte Aufsätze 1933–1969*, ed. E. Grässer et al. (Marburg: N. G. Elwert Verlag, 1965), pp. 15–35. On p. 110 (in the reprint, 19), for example, Kümmel states: "For the rigid concept of a law code . . . was never the Jewish notion of the law. The Jewish idea of the law is instead always embedded in the more inclusive ideas of tradition." This statement must be qualified, however, because of the Sadducees.

12. See, for example, Matt. 5:43.

13. The introduction has been expanded by a redactor in Mark 7:1b, 3–4; the same is true of vv. 14–23, in which, besides the saying of the Lord in v. 15, other traditions, significantly later, have been incorporated. Matthew reworked the entire text. See Erich Klostermann, *Das Markusevangelium*, HNT 3 (4th ed., 1950), pp. 66 ff.; also Martin Dibelius, *From Tradition to Gospel*, trans. B. L. Woolf (New York: Scribner's, 1935, reprint 1965), pp. 220–21; Kümmel, "Jesus und . . . Traditionsgedanke" (cited above, n. 11), pp. 28 ff.

men. Jesus' opponents look on these ordinances as "tradition of the elders" and binding interpretation of the law; Jesus disqualifies them as the work of man (Mark 7:5, 8). The consequence for sacral cultic ordinances is formulated most trenchantly in Mark 7:15: "Nothing that goes into a man from outside can defile him; no, it is the things that come out of him that defile him." There is nothing parallel or analogous to this statement in all of Jewish literature. Its significance has been strikingly expounded by Ernst Käsemann: ". . . the man who denies that impurity from external sources can penetrate into man's essential being is striking at the presuppositions and the plain verbal sense of the Torah and at the authority of Moses himself. Over and above that, he is striking at the presuppositions of the whole classical conception of cultus with its sacrificial and expiatory system. To put this in another way, he is removing the distinction (which is fundamental to the whole of ancient thought) between the *temenos,* the realm of the sacred, and the secular, and it is for this reason that he is able to consort with sinners." [14] It is thus not merely casuistic interpretation of the law that is the target of Jesus' criticism, but the law itself. In like manner, the antitheses (Matt. 5:21–48) and the divorce pericope (Mark 10:1–9 and parallels) attack Moses himself, an attack that would be tantamount to blasphemy for a devout Jew. Such conduct is comprehensible only because Jesus acts with the authority of God working eschatologically.

14. E. Käsemann, *Essays* (cited above, n. 8) , p. 39.

How much any way of life oriented toward formal obedience to the law is affected is shown by Jesus' views on fasting. In Matthew 6:16–18, the primary point is not the contrast between the outward and the secret, but the fact that all fasting must stand in the sign of joy. In Judaism fasting was an expression of grief and penance;[15] fasting as an expression of thankfulness and joy was unknown. That Jesus is not merely attacking hypocritical fasting is shown by the controversy story (Streitgespräch) in Mark 2:18, 19*a*: the saving event that begins with Jesus' message and ministry spells an end to fasting in the traditional sense.[16] The metaphors of the "bridegroom" and the "wedding guests" point unmistakably to the dawning age of salvation. Joy is a part of the wedding celebration; therefore eating and drinking in joyous thanksgiving is proper.

These considerations also cast light on Jesus' repasts or meals of celebration. It was no gratuitous reproach to accuse Jesus of being a "glutton and drunkard," in contrast to the ascetic Baptist. Even worse, he was a "friend of tax collectors and sinners" (Matt. 11:19/Luke 7:34). For Jesus had table fellowship not with a circle of the elect, but with whoever would follow his call; he made a particular point of inviting the rejected and unclean to dine with him.

15. Judaism also knew (regular) fasting as an exercise of devotion and as substitutionary; cf. Luke 18:12. For a discussion of fasting, see J. Behm, *"nēstis, nēsteuō,"* in *TDNT*, Vol. 4, pp. 924–35.

16. The original text of the controversy story is found only in Mark 2:18, 19*a*. The appended metaphors in vv. 21–22 have the same intent, while vv. 19*b*, 20 are a later insertion, introducing the notion of fasting out of grief for Jesus' death. In addition to the historical-critical commentaries, see the discussion of J. Jeremias, *"nymphē,* etc.," in *TDNT*, Vol. 4, pp. 1103, 1105.

It is to them that God shows his salvation, and therefore to them that Jesus directs his ministry: "It is not the healthy that need a doctor, but the sick" (Mark 2:17a). The miraculous feeding of the multitude, in which Jesus assists the poor in their distress,[17] belongs in the same context. Like the wedding, table fellowship was a standard image for the time of salvation, and Jesus' repasts are nothing less than anticipations of the eschatological heavenly banquet. Jesus' farewell meal in Jerusalem is also intended to be understood from this perspective, for Mark 14:25 is a promise of the heavenly fulfillment of Jesus' table fellowship.[18] Jesus' repasts thus reveal quite concretely the significance of his conduct with respect to the liturgical ordinances of Judaism: here all ritual precepts are set aside by virtue of sovereign authority, all walls separating the sacred from the profane are torn down. These acts of table fellowship take place in the midst of daily life, and no one remains excluded from the act of worship.[19]

Revealing, too, are Jesus' statements about prayer.[20] Prayer always occupied an outstanding place in the

17. On this point, see my article "Die alttestamentlichen Motive in der urchristlichen Abendmahlsüberlieferung," *EvT* 27 (1967): 337–74; also Alkuin Heising, *Die Botschaft der Brotvermehrung*, SBib 15 (1966).

18. On this point, too, see my comments in "Motive" (cited above, n. 17), pp. 344 ff., 347 ff.

19. Very typical is the parable about a banquet in Luke 14:16–24 (Matt. 22:1–14), with its summoning of guests from the streets and squares of the city, as well as the highways and hedgerows.

20. See J. Herrmann and H. Greeven, "*euchomai*," in *TDNT*, Vol. 2, pp. 775–808 (with bibliography); also the essay by J. Jeremias, "Daily Prayer in the Life of Jesus and the Primitive Church," Eng. trans. Christoph Burchard in Jeremias' *The Prayers of Jesus*, SBT 2/6 (1967), pp. 66–81, although dependence on Jewish prayer practice is overemphasized.

cultic tradition of Israel. For Jesus, too, it is central
to the life of any man called and favored by God.
But just as Matthew 6:16–18 does more than attack
an outward show of fasting, so Matthew 6:5–8 does
more than attack an outward show of prayer: as the
charge of *polylogia* (v. 7, "many words") above all
indicates, it is the fundamental view of prayer as a
pious work that is under attack. For Jesus, prayer
cannot be anything other than an expression of confidence. This is the basis on which his astonishing
statements about assurance that prayer will be heard
must be understood. Above all the statement about
the faith that moves mountains bespeaks the worshiper's unreserved confidence in God's miraculous
intervention;[21] the same is true of the closely associated statement: "Whatever you ask fo. in prayer,
(only) have faith that you will receive it and it will
be yours" (Mark 11:24).[22] The invocation of God
as "Abba," so striking within the context of contemporary Judaism, is also an expression of confi-

21. This logion is found on the one hand in Mark 11:22–23 and
parallels, on the other in its Q recension in Luke 17:6/Matt. 17:20.
This is not the place to discuss the tradition-historical problems in
detail. Interestingly, in the preaching of Jesus, faith in the sense of
unreserved confidence is mentioned only in the context of prayer
and miracles. On the question of "faith and prayer," see Bornkamm, *Jesus* (cited above, n. 3), pp. 129 ff.; Gerhard Ebeling,
"Jesus and Faith," in his *Word and Faith*, trans. J. W. Leitch
(Philadelphia: Fortress, 1963), pp. 201–46, especially pp. 227 ff. and
232 ff.

22. Typical also is the appended saying Mark 11:25, a later trans-
formation of Matt. 5:23–24 (see below, p. 25), a saying concerning
reconciliation, into a saying about prayer. The fifth petition of the
Lord's Prayer shows that this accords with Jesus' views. Just as one
confidently hopes for everything from the Father, so one must forgive one's fellowman everything on the basis of the mercy one has
oneself been shown. The parable in Matt. 18:23–35 stands in the
background.

dence. The particular meaning of this "Abba" has been elucidated by recent scholarship.[23] We are dealing with a word borrowed from the language of children and the family;[24] it signifies that man no longer addresses a God distant and exalted, but can experience the immediate nearness of God, who has begun his eschatological work, and therefore may say "Abba" with unrestrained devotion.[25] Undoubtedly "a special relationship with God" is here expressed.[26] Furthermore, Jesus not only prayed to God in this manner himself,[27] but also authorized his followers to use this form of address. The Lord's Prayer [28] is nothing more

23. See above all J. Jeremias, "Abba," in his *Prayers of Jesus* (cited above, n. 20), pp. 11–65; W. Marchel, *Abba Père! La prière du Christ et des Chrétiens*, AnBib 19 (1961).

24. The form is not an Aramaic *status emphaticus*, but babytalk; see Jeremias, "Abba" (cited above, n. 23), pp. 58–59. On pp. 60–62, however, Jeremias rightly points out that the word was not borrowed directly from children's language, but had long had a place in the intimate language of the family.

25. The form of address in Matt. 6:9 incontestably represents a return to Jewish practice.

26. Jeremias, "Abba" (cited above, n. 23), p. 62.

27. Apart from the cry of prayer on the cross, which goes back to Ps. 22:1, all the prayers of Jesus that have come down to us contain an address to the Father: the cry of joy in Matt. 11:25–26 and parallel; the Gethsemane prayer in Mark 14:36 and parallels; and the Lord's Prayer; the same is true in John 11:41; 12:27; and 17:1, albeit these are not authentic sayings of Jesus (above all the idea of "praying in Jesus' name" found in John 14:14 and *passim* cannot go back to Jesus himself).

28. See Gustaf Dalman, *Die Worte Jesu* (2d ed., 1930), Vol. 1, pp. 283–365 (not included in Eng. trans.); E. Lohmeyer, *Our Father,* trans. John Bowden (New York: Harper & Row, 1966) (=*The Lord's Prayer* [London: Collins, 1965]); K. G. Kuhn, *Achtzehngebet und Vaterunser und der Reim,* Wissenschaftliche Untersuchungen zum Neuen Testament, 1 (Tübingen: Mohr, 1950); Heinz Schürmann, *Praying with Christ,* trans. W. M. Ducey and A. Simon (New York: Herder & Herder, 1964); J. Jeremias, *The Lord's Prayer,* trans. J. Reumann, FBBS 8 (3d ed. rev., 1969), reprinted in Jeremias's *Prayers of Jesus* (cited above, n. 20), pp. 82–107; idem, "Vaterunser," in *RGG,* Vol. 6, cols. 1235–37.

or less than a development of the cry "Abba," and the concerns of the prayer correspond to the promise of eschatological salvation. Luke preserved the earlier short version of the Lord's Prayer, although Matthew preserved more details of the original wording. The two " 'Thou'-petitions," for the hallowing of God's name and the coming of his kingdom, are linked with three "We-petitions," which show clearly that the first two petitions are not imploring God's expected eschatological action in the traditional sense; they are the petitions of men who know that God's reign is beginning, and may therefore in the present moment pray for the bread of the age of salvation, as well as forgiveness and deliverance from eschatological affliction.[29] Attention must be given not only to the content but also to the outward form of the Lord's Prayer in its original version: it is not a prayer in Hebrew but in the Aramaic vernacular—not totally out of the question in contemporary Judaism, but unusual. This means again that Jesus "removes prayer from the liturgical sphere of sacral language and places it right in the midst of everyday life." [30] This lends force to the observation that Jesus was not bound by the fixed times and prescribed forms of prayer.[31]

---

29. For a discussion of all the details, above all the difficult term *"epiousios,"* I refer merely to Jeremias, *The Lord's Prayer* (cited above, n. 28), pp. 21 ff. (in *Prayers of Jesus*, pp. 98 ff.).
30. Jeremias, *Prayers of Jesus* (cited above, n. 20), p. 76.
31. See Jeremias, ibid., pp. 75 ff. The evidence cited on pp. 73–75 that Jesus at the same time observed the traditional times of prayer is not, in my opinion, totally convincing. All that can be demonstrated is Jesus' reference to the Shema—which, however, is rightly distinguished from the tradition of prayer (pp. 67–69).

Of special significance is Jesus' conduct with respect
to the temple. The story of Jesus in the temple at
the age of twelve is irrelevant here. What we must
examine is how to judge Jesus' participation in the
Jewish pilgrimage festivals. According to the Synoptic
account,[32] Jesus came to Jerusalem only once, at the
end of his life, to celebrate Passover; Johannine tradition,[33] however, makes us think in terms of several
journeys of Jesus to Jerusalem. There is no certain
evidence that Jesus celebrated a Passover meal,[34] and
there is no mention of any participation in the temple
cult. Jesus preaches within the temple precincts and
disputes with his opponents.[35] In addition, there is
criticism of priests and Levites in the parable of the
good Samaritan (Luke 10:30 ff.), and the practice of
corban is condemned in Mark 7:9–13.[36] If explicit

32. Mark 10:1, 32; 11:1 ff. and parallels.

33. John 2:13 ff. (Passover); 5:1 ff. (*heortē,* "a feast," probably
another Passover festival; see Rudolf Bultmann, *The Gospel of
John: A Commentary,* trans. G. R. Beasley-Murray et al. [Philadel-
phia: Westminster, 1971], p. 240); 7:1 ff., 14 ff. (Feast of Booths);
10:22 ff. (Feast of Dedication); 11:55 ff. (Passover). Various types
of traditional material have here been combined redactionally;
there is no basis for any historical outline of Jesus' life involving a
ministry of several years.

34. I refer here merely to my discussion in "Motive" (cited above,
n. 17), p. 343. As is well known, other scholars hold the contrary
opinion: J. Jeremias, *The Eucharistic Words of Jesus,* trans. Nor-
man Perrin (New York: Scribner's, 1966), pp. 41 ff.; H. Schürmann,
"Abendmahl I. A.," in *Lexikon für Theologie und Kirche* (Freiburg: Herder, 2d ed.), Vol. 1, pp. 27–35; Eugen Ruckstuhl,
Chronology of the Last Days of Jesus, trans. V. J. Drapela (New
York: Desclée, 1965), pp. 17 ff.

35. According to Mark 11:1 ff. and Luke 19:29 ff., Jesus healed no
one during his stay in Jerusalem; in a brief summary statement,
Matt. 21:14 mentions healings in the temple precincts. The situation differs in John: apart from the healing of the cripple in 5:1 ff.,
the raising of Lazarus is tantamount to being the cause of Jesus'
passion: 11:45 ff.; 12:9 ff., 17 ff.

36. The corban oath was a way of dedicating something as a votive
offering to the temple. It was much utilized in disputes over

recognition of the temple and priesthood is to be found anywhere, it is in the narratives at Luke 17:1–19 and Mark 1:40–44 and parallels, where lepers are told to go to Jerusalem and show themselves to the priests; but one must note that the priests exercised legal functions with respect to the lepers: only their verdict could annul the sequestration to which the lepers were condemned. Furthermore, the point of the first instance is that the lepers who had asked Jesus to help them placed their faith in him, and thereupon experienced a cure while they were still on their way to the priests. In the other instance, however, the cure came first; and the command, "Make the offering laid down by Moses for your cleansing," can in fact give the impression that Jesus is here requiring a cultic act. But the emphasis of the command is on the concluding *eis martyrion autois*, "for a testimony to them," which must be understood, as in Mark 6:11; 13:9, as incriminating testimony: the very priests who confirm the cleansing and accept the usual offering recognize the cure worked by Jesus, thereby condemning their own unbelief. Thus this text, too, is to be understood as intending criticism of the representatives of the temple cult.[37]

Mark 12:41–44 and parallel does not bear directly on the problem of the temple. The point of the story

inheritances and support cases. Since this oath was considered irrevocable, its use led to all sorts of uncharitableness, which was tolerated and even promoted by the temple priesthood. See K. H. Rengstorf, "*korban,*" in *TDNT*, Vol. 3, pp. 860–66.

37. In this context we cannot discuss in detail the extent to which Mark 1:40–44 and parallels record an original saying of Jesus as opposed to a particular interpretation on the part of the community. [1:44, as understood above, is to be rendered "for a proof *against* the *priests,*" not (as in RSV) "for a proof *to* the *people.*—Ed.]

about the widow's mite is the readiness of this woman
to give away all that she has: where it takes place is
irrelevant. It is more reasonable to ask whether the
saying about readiness to be reconciled in Matthew
5:23–24 does not yield a positive estimation of the
temple cult.[38] If the worshiper is commanded to make
peace with his brother before offering his gift, proper
participation in the sacrificial cult of the temple is
apparently being required. But this is a modern conclusion; here, too, it is impossible to overlook the
open declaration of war on the cult. If the temple
cult is man's approach before the face of God, proper
performance of the prescribed ritual is all that matters. Anyone who interrupts performance of the ritual
to make peace with his brother bears witness that
there is something that matters more than sacrifice.[39]

Jesus' claim to be able to forgive sins goes consid-
erably further. The accusation of blasphemy brought
against Jesus in Mark 2:5 ff. is not without reason.
According to the Jewish view, the right to forgive
sins is reserved to God alone; only in the temple cult,
established by God's gracious ordinance, can men
receive forgiveness for particular transgressions.[40]
Jesus, however, promises men eschatological forgiveness of sins, thus abrogating the propitiatory system

38. For a discussion of Matt. 5:23–24, see J. Jeremias, " 'Lass allda
deine Gabe'," in his *Abba: Studien zur neutestamentlichen Theologie und Zeitgeschichte* (Göttingen: Vandenhoeck & Ruprecht,
1966), pp. 103–7.

39. In this version the saying is much more pointed than in Mark
11:25 (see p. 20, with n. 22): Matt. 5:23–24 requires something
that runs counter to the law; Mark 11:25 is concerned with the
proper attitude during prayer and conduct toward one's neighbor.

40. See von Rad, *Theology* (cited above, Chap. II, n. 5), Vol. 1,
pp. 241 ff.; K. Koch, "Sühne und Sündenvergebung um die Wende
von der exilischen zur nachexilischen Zeit," *EvT* 26 (1966): 217–39;
also my discussion in "Motive" (cited above, n. 17), pp. 358 ff.

of the temple.[41] This explains why the post-Easter
community could say not only, "What is here is
greater than Jonah, what is here is greater than Solomon," but also, "What is here is greater than the
temple." [42]

Jesus' attitude toward the temple cult was expressed
most pointedly in his saying concerning the temple
and his eschatological symbolic action in the outer
court of the temple. The saying is recorded in six
different versions, but nowhere in its original form.[43]
The sixfold tradition, however, permits us to draw
certain conclusions. Despite Mark 13:2 and Acts 6:14,
the logion must have comprised two members; furthermore, as can still be seen from Mark 13:2, its
original formulation was probably passive, that is, it
spoke of an act performed by God.[44] The protasis
spoke of the destruction of "this temple," the apodo-

---

41. The forgiveness of sins has more significance in Jesus' ministry
than the number of texts suggests. This is shown by the petition
for forgiveness in the Lord's Prayer and the parable in Matt.
18:23–25, as well as Mark 2:5 and Luke 7:48. But table fellowship
with sinners is also an expression of the forgiveness of sins. In addition, Jesus' healing miracles are probably all meant to be understood in this light, even when the narratives in part represent very
different points of view. There is furthermore the indirect evidence of the authorization of the disciples to forgive sins: Matt.
16:19; 18:18; John 20:23.

42. See on the one hand Matt. 12:41–42/Luke 11:31–32, on the
other the secondary expansion added to the narrative of the
disciples' plucking grain: the example of the priests is added to
the example of David, together with the saying "What is here is
greater than the temple" and the quotation from Hos. 6:6 (also
found in Matt. 9:13).

43. Mark 13:2 (cf. *varia lectio*); 14:58; 15:29; Matt. 26:61; Acts
6:14; John 2:19 (omitting identical parallels).

44. The later versions speak of an act performed by Jesus when he
comes again (Acts 6:14; Mark 15:29; Matt. 26:61); in Mark 14:58
the saying has been reinterpreted ecclesiologically, in John 2:19
christologically (see below, p. 61).

sis of its restoration in the course of three days, the
period of three days signifying a short eschatological
space of time.[45] The notion of an eschatological destruction of the earthly temple and the building of
a new heavenly temple was as such not totally alien to
contemporary Judaism, although hope that the temple would stand forever probably predominated.[46]
What gave the saying its immediate point, however,
was its association with Jesus' symbolic act in the
outer court of the temple and his claim that his action
marked the end of the Jerusalem temple. The saying
concerning the temple and the symbolic act belong
together by virtue of their subject matter, although
their direct association in John 2:13–22 is secondary.[47] The term "cleansing of the temple" should not
be used, since it refers not to the actual event in the
past but to a later understanding of what took place.[48]

45. The terms "destroy," "this temple," "build," and "in three days"
remain constant. For a discussion of individual problems, see R. A.
Hoffmann, "Das Wort Jesu von der Zerstörung und dem Wiederauf-
bau des Tempels," in *Neutestamentliche Studien Georg Heinrici
. . . ,* Untersuchungen zum Neuen Testament, 6 (Leipzig: Hinrichs,
1914), pp. 130–39; P. Vielhauer, *Oikodome* (Diss., Heidelberg, 1939),
pp. 62 ff.; E. Lohmeyer, *Das Evangelium des Markus,* KEK 1/2
(15th ed., 1959), pp. 326–27.

46. On this point we refer on the one hand to apocalypticism, on
the other to the Zealots or the "War Scroll" from Qumran (1QM).

47. For an analysis of the text see in particular Bultmann, *John*
(cited above, n. 33), pp. 122 ff.; E. Haenchen, "Johanneische Probleme," *ZTK* 56 (1959): 19–54, especially pp. 34 ff., 42 ff., reprinted
in his collected essays, *Gott und Mensch* (Tübingen: Mohr, 1965),
pp. 78–113, especially 95–105; R. Schnackenburg, *Das Johannesevangelium,* Vol. 1 (1965), pp. 359 ff. (in English, *The Gospel
According to John,* trans. K. Smyth [New York: Herder, 1968–],
only Vol. 1 has appeared). Further, Raymond E. Brown, S. S., *The
Gospel According to John,* 2 vols., Anchor Bible 29, 29A (Garden
City: Doubleday, 1966–70), Vol. 1, pp. 114–25.

48. E. Haenchen (*Der Weg Jesu: Eine Erklärung des Markus-
Evangeliums und der kanonischen Parallelen* [Berlin: de Gruyter,
1966], p. 388) asserts that the notion of a cleansing of the temple

The key word dominating the recorded tradition is *ekballein,* "drive out," so that the designation "expulsion from the temple" is more apposite in any case. What Jesus did in the temple precincts undoubtedly belongs to the end of his ministry, and clearly led directly to the events of his passion.[49] As not only John 2:13–22 but also Mark 11:15–17, 27b–33 show, expulsion from the temple and the question of authority constitute a unit,[50] and were very probably behind the decision of the Council in Mark 14:1–2. In the expulsion from the temple itself we must distinguish the account of what Jesus did from the associated Old Testament interpretaments.[51] Jesus limits his actions to the outer precincts of the temple, the court of the Gentiles, where sale of sacrificial animals and exchange of currency were allowed. Jesus expels buyers, sellers, and animals, overturns the tables of the money-changers, and scatters their money.[52] But the significance of his actions extends

was introduced by exegesis. This claim is not quite accurate, in that initial hints of this understanding are already found in the primitive Christian tradition; but under no circumstances must this interpretation be taken as a point of departure.

49. This is not the place to examine the historical problems in more detail. In John 2, this event and the narrative of the wedding at Cana have been placed programmatically at the beginning of Jesus' ministry.

50. Mark 11:12–14, 20–25 is an independent complex of tradition; the transitions in Mark 11:11, 18–19, 27a are redactional. In John 2:18 ff. the question of authority is associated with a demand for a sign; the saying concerning the temple and testimony of the resurrection are also incorporated.

51. We can restrict our attention to the traditions in Mark 11:15–17 and John 2:13–22. Matt. 21:12–13 contains only a few minor changes; Luke 19:45–46 is an extreme condensation. Specifically Markan is the phrase *pasin tois ethnesin,* "for all the nations" (11:17).

52. The Markan and Johannine traditions do not agree in detail: Mark 11:15 mentions sellers and buyers, John 2:14 the sellers with

beyond the outer court; it affects the entire temple.[53]
For Jesus' actions make the traditional sacrificial cult
impossible.[54] From the Jewish point of view, we have
to do with an act of sacrilege; Jesus is therefore asked
what his legitimation is, and he refuses to answer.[55]
It is out of place to speculate how Jesus could con-
trive to accomplish what he did;[56] we are dealing
with nothing more than a symbolic act of limited extent; but as such it takes on its full weight, and it was
understood in this sense. The Jerusalem temple is
part of the old aeon that is passing away, and the
sacrificial cult must give way to the kingdom of God
that is dawning—this is demonstrated for all to see.
The post-Easter community then associated various
quotations with the traditional narrative to interpret
it.[57] The charge, taken from Jeremiah 7:11, that the
temple has been made a *spēlaion lēstōn* ("den of rob-
bers") still reveals the original force of Jesus' act most

their sheep and cattle. The latter probably belonged to the original
narrative, the more so since sellers of pigeons are mentioned in
both instances. Both traditions also mention overturning the tables
of the money-changers. On the formula *ta te probata kai tous boas*,
"the sheep and the oxen" (2:15), see C. K. Barrett, *The Gospel
according to St. John* (New York: Macmillan, 1955), p. 165.

53. *Pace* E. Lohmeyer, "Die Reinigung des Tempels," *ThBl* 20
(1941): 257–64; and idem, *Lord of the Temple* (cited above, Chap.
I, n. 7), p, 39. According to Lohmeyer, the passage deals "only indirectly with a Jewish Temple problem, but much more directly
with the problem of the 'Gentiles'."

54. J. Wellhausen already pointed out (*Das Evangelium Marci*
[Berlin: Reimer, 2d ed., 1909], p. 90) that Jesus' appearance in
the temple "in fact probably was even more significant than is
usually assumed."

55. Mark 11:27–33 and parallels.

56. The question has recently been raised once more by Haenchen,
Weg (cited above, n. 48), p. 384; W. Grundmann, *Das Evangelium
des Markus*, THK 1 (2d ed., 1959), p. 230.

57. The quotation is clearly set apart in Mark 11:17a, and likewise
in John 2:17.

clearly; for *lēstēs* means "thief" and "murderer." This is of course immediately attenuated and understood as in John 2:16b: "You must not turn my Father's house into a market."[58] Here, as in the statement in Mark 11:16 that Jesus refused to allow the temple to be used as a thoroughfare,[59] the way is paved for an understanding that moves in the direction of a cleansing of the temple. This tendency was finally reinforced positively by quotation of Isaiah 56:7 (*ho oikos mou oikos proseuchēs klēthēsetai,* "my house shall be called a house of prayer") in Mark 11:17b and parallels.[60] The Johannine text exhibits less interest in the temple than in the personal consequences for Jesus; the quotation from Psalm 69:10 hints that zeal for the house of God will "devour" Jesus, i.e., bring about his death.[61]

When we look back over Jesus' ministry, we see two fundamental points in his relationship to Jewish worship: he repudiates Jewish observance of the law

58. Quite typical is the phrase *ho oikos tou patros mou,* "my Father's house." John no longer records any Old Testament quotation; what is left of the reference refers less to Jer. 7:11 than to Zech. 14:21. See C. H. Dodd, *Historical Tradition in the Fourth Gospel* (New York: Cambridge University Press, 1963), pp. 159–60.

59. We are dealing here with the Jewish principle that carrying goods through the temple would infringe the sanctity of the temple; see Klostermann, *Markusevangelium* (cited above, n. 13), p. 117.

60. The phrase *pasin tois ethnesin,* "for all the nations," likewise taken over from Isa. 56:7, agrees with the universalistic tendency of Mark; see my book *Mission in the New Testament,* trans. F. Clarke, SBT 47 (1965), pp. 111–20, especially 115–16. As Matthew and Luke show, it probably did not belong to the tradition in its original form.

61. John 2:17 must be understood in this sense, not in the sense of being inwardly "consumed." See Schnackenburg, *Johannesevangelium* (cited above, n. 47), pp. 362–63. Thus the passion reference in verse 17 parallels the resurrection reference in verse 22, albeit the former cites scripture, the latter Jesus' own words.

and its concomitant ritualization of life, and he pro-
claims the end of the temple cult. This means that
the sovereign kingship of God abolishes the sacral
cultic order of the Old Testament.[62] This is possible
because with the coming of God's sovereign kingship
man is bound directly to God's will, and can therefore serve him in joy and thanksgiving. In this context the twofold law of love reveals its unity and its
critical function: there can be love for God only
where there is also room for love for one's neighbor
and enemy, but love for God and for one's fellowman
are not simply identified. At the same time all partic-
ularism is vanquished: God's claim extends to the
entire world. Therefore Jesus can expect men to
gather from all corners of the earth (Matt. 8:11/Luke
13:28–29).

62. Under no circumstances is it accurate to characterize Jesus'
attitude by reference to the prophets' criticism of sacrifice, suggest-
ing a "spiritualization" of the sacrificial concepts; *pace* Leipoldt,
Gottesdienst (cited above, Chap. I, n. 2), pp. 10 ff.

IV

The Foundations
of Early Christian Worship

Early Christian worship represents a new beginning. We can comprehend its uniqueness only when we take into account its fundamental postulates as the essential factors behind the innovation. Here, too, we can speak of constraint and freedom, but constraint does not mean dependence on specific forms of Jewish worship. The disciples are bound to Jesus' ministry and the ongoing eschatological events; therein lies their freedom. Only secondarily, then, does the question of Jewish worship arise; its radical modification is especially noteworthy. It is therefore by no means sufficient to point out similarities and differences in detail; the specific elements and the reasons for them must be determined.

What links primitive Christianity with Judaism is, as in the case of Jesus, confession of the one God who created heaven and earth. There is further the assurance that this God is now acting on the basis of his promises spoken by the prophets, and is acting with the intention of realizing salvation for all the world. It is characteristic that no institutional separation from Judaism results; there are not two "confessional groups" or "religious communities" confronting each other, but the community of salvation as the true Israel that summons the ancient people of God to repent and acknowledge the eschatological saving act of God. Official separation between Judaism and Christianity did not take place until the end of the first century, and was instigated primarily by Judaism,[1] not Christianity. Initially, therefore, we must say that the worship of the early church was built on the same foundation as Jewish worship of God. This explains why even missionary preaching to the Gentiles presupposes belief in God in the sense of the Old Testament tradition.[2]

This constraint imposed by the fundamental confession of Israel is intertwined, however, with a freedom toward all previous requirements, because the message, and therefore also the faith and worship of the Christians, is concerned with the newness of God's eschatological acts. Indisputable as the common presuppositions are, in the light of the eschaton not only is a new understanding achieved of God's past actions and his promises, but what is eschatologically new imposes itself in concrete form, taking hold of what is old and reshaping it.

Three factors are essential for the primitive community: Jesus' own message and ministry; the death, resurrection, and presence of Christ; and the opera-

1. The *birkath hamminim*, i.e., the introduction of a special petition against Christian heretics in the "Eighteen Benedictions" (*Shemoneh Esreh*), played a crucial role. See Bousset-Gressmann, *Religion* (cited above, Chap. II, n. 20), p. 177; Goppelt, *Apostolic . . . Times* (cited above, Chap. I, n. 5), pp. 118 ff.
2. See the pre-Pauline formula in 1 Thess. 1:9*b*, 10 and the two missionary addresses to Gentiles in Acts 14:15–17 and 17:22–31. See the detailed discussion in Ulrich Wilckens, *Die Missionsreden der Apostelgeschichte*, WMANT 5 (2d ed., 1963), pp. 80 ff.

tion of the Holy Spirit. The onset of the eschatological events is indissolubly linked to the appearance of
Jesus and his pre-Easter ministry. The message will
henceforth always be associated with him as the
bringer of salvation. His disciples had been expressly
commissioned to proclaim his message and continue
his work.[3] But his death appeared to call all this into
question. The significance of Jesus' dying had to be
deduced step by step on the basis of the Old Testament after life had been brought forth through his
death. The event of Jesus' resurrection as a proleptic
raising of the dead, whereby Jesus became the "first
fruits of the dead,"[4] made it clear that the decisive
victory over the powers of sin and death and over
the world had now been achieved. The message of
Jesus' death and resurrection therefore did not
merely take its place alongside Jesus' own message;
henceforth the proclamation of salvation's irruption
and of Jesus' earthly ministry could be made only
from the perspective of the cross and Easter. That
God's eschatological activity demonstrated his immediate power was now experienced by the faithful primarily through the outpouring and operation of the
Holy Spirit. It is true that the gift of the Spirit was
understood as "earnest money,"[5] and unrestricted

3. See the accounts of how the disciples are sent forth in Mark
6:7–13; Matt. 9:35–11:1; Luke 9:1–6; 10:1–16. The missionary commandment of the risen Lord in Mark 16:15–16, 19–20 and Matt.
28:18–20 places the commission in the light of the Easter event.
See my book *Mission* (cited above, Chap. III, n. 60), pp. 41–46 and
61 ff.

4. 1 Cor. 15:20: *aparchē tōn kekoimēmenōn.* Cf. Col. 1:18; Acts
26:23; but also 1 Cor. 6:14; 2 Cor. 4:14; Rom. 8:11.

5. 2 Cor. 1:22: *arrabōn tou pneumatos,* "the 'guarantee' which the
Spirit is"; cf. Eph. 1:14 and Rom. 8:23: *aparchē tou pneumatos,*
"the first fruits, the Spirit."

bestowal of the Spirit was not expected until some future date; but this earnest money of the Spirit, which strengthened the faithful, guided them, and equipped them for service, had already been given them. This made possible an actual sense of community.[6]

The irruption of the eschaton, which was already taking place in the old aeon, made it impossible simply to adopt the worship of Judaism. Not only had Jesus himself breached and abrogated the traditional cultic order, a fact that the primitive community could not escape; it was the present reality of God's eschatological activity that demanded new forms of worship.[7] Individual changes were undertaken with varying intensity. There were circles in the primitive community that adhered much more closely to Jewish tradition than others; but nowhere could one ignore the fact that what mattered was no longer the law and a promise for the future: now the saving and fulfilling act of God in Christ was the focus of attention for the community as it offered praise, thanksgiving, and intercession.

Nothing bespeaks the novelty of Christian worship so plainly as the terminology employed for its concepts. Almost none of the traditional concepts occur in the New Testament; and where they do, they are

6. We cite merely the bibliography in Eduard Schweizer, *"pneuma,"* in *TDNT,* Vol. 6, pp. 396 ff.

7. It may remain an open question whether the presence of God's eschatological activity was conceived primarily christologically or pneumatologically. It was not until relatively late in the history of primitive Christianity that Christology and pneumatology were clearly coordinated.

unmistakably used metaphorically. Cultic terminology is consciously avoided for Christian worship; it serves only to characterize the temple worship of the Old Testament, and to describe the Christ-event or the conduct of Christians in the world.[8] The only term that occurs with a certain regularity is *synerchesthai* ("come together") or *synagesthai* ("be gathered together").[9] The "coming together" of the faithful is the significant feature of Christian worship; and where the community comes together, God is praised, his mighty acts are proclaimed, prayers are said, and the Lord's Supper is celebrated. All other terms appear only incidentally. *Latreia* refers to Jewish worship or, in the context of Pauline parenesis, the offering of one's body as *logikē latreia* ("spirtual worship").[10] The verb *latreuein,* "serve," it is true, is somewhat more widely distributed; but it is not limited to worship, and is sometimes used in deliberate antithesis to cultic and ritual tradition.[11] The

8. For a more detailed discussion of this point see below, pp. 59 ff.

9. See especially 1 Cor. 11:17, 20, 33–34; 14:23, 26; the epistle of Ignatius to the Ephesians 13:1, as well as Matt. 18–20; Acts 4:31; 20:7–8 and 14:27; 15:6; 1 Cor. 5:4; Didache 16:2; also *synagōgē* in James 2:2, *episynagōgē* in Heb. 10:25, and *synaxis* in 1 Clem. 34:7; Justin's *Apology* 1. 65.

10. For the first sense in the New Testament, see Rom. 9:4; Heb. 9:1, 6; also John 16:2; for the second sense, Rom. 12:1. *Latreia* corresponds to the Old Testament ʿᵃbōda; see O. Cullmann, *Urchristentum und Gottesdienst,* ATANT 3 (2d ed., 1950), p. 11, n. 1 (the note is not included in the Eng. trans. cited above, Chap. I, n. 2).

11. It stands for the Old Testament cult in Luke 1:74; 2:37; Acts 7:7, 42; and Hebrews *passim*; it is used in the general sense in Matt. 4:10/Luke 4:8; Rom. 1:25; and elsewhere. It is used in contrast to the Jewish Old Testament tradition in Phil. 3:3 (in contrast to circumcision): *hoi pneumati theou latreuontes,* we "who worship God in the Spirit"; Heb. 12:28: *latreuōmen euarestōs* (!) *tō theō,* "let us offer acceptable worship (!) to God"; also Rom. 1:9: *hō* (sc. *theō*) *latreuō . . . en tō euangeliō tou huiou autou,* God "whom I serve . . . in the gospel of his Son" (cf. Rom. 15:16, discussed in the next note).

same is true of *leitourgia* and *leitourgein,* "service" and "serve," which never occur as special terms for worship, so that they can refer to the missionary proclamation of the gospel, the collection, and even the state's function which is appointed by God.[12] *Thrēskeia* ("worship, religion"), too, is no longer used for worship in the narrow sense. It can be applied to the Old Testament cult and the angel worship of the Colossian heretics;[13] but only in James 1:27 does it appear with reference to the Christian community: "Service that is without spot or stain before God and the Father is this: to go to the help of orphans and widows in their distress, and keep oneself untarnished by the world." Above all, *thysia* ("sacri-

---

12. In Luke 1:23; Heb. 8:2; 9:21; 10:11 *leitourgia, leitourgein,* and *leitourgos* refer to the Old Testament cult; in Phil. 2:25, 30, to the service of Epaphroditus; in 2 Cor. 9:12; Rom. 15:27, to the collection for Jerusalem; in Rom. 13:6, to the duties of state officials. In Heb. 8:6 it is used christologically. Rom. 15:16 is especially instructive: there Paul refers to himself as *leitourgos Christou Iēsou eis ta ethnē,* "a minister of Christ Jesus to the Gentiles," and characterizes his task as priestly service to the gospel of God, with the goal of "offering the Gentiles" to God as an "acceptable" sacrifice, that is, "consecrated by the Holy Spirit." Here the various terms from sacrificial and cultic language are removed from their original sphere of meaning and applied to missionary service. Phil. 2:17*a* also belongs in this context: what was termed *hierourgein to euangelion tou theou* ("perform priestly service to the gospel of God") in Rom. 15:16 is here referred to as *thysia kai leitourgia tēs pisteōs hymōn,* "a sacrifice and service of your faith," that is, the passage deals with sacrifice and service *on behalf of* the faith of the Philippian community, and Paul compares the death he may be facing to the offering of blood in the cult; for, thanks to the propitiatory and salvific force of the gospel, his entire apostolic ministry has come to take the place once occupied by the cult. Only in Acts 13:2 do we find the term in the specific sense of worship: *leitourgountes tō kyriō kai nēsteuontes,* "worshiping the Lord and fasting." But this, especially in connection with Christian fasting, is characteristic of the idea of worship toward the close of the first century (apart from Luke 2:37, see also Mark 9:29 *varia lectio;* Acts 13:3; 14:23; and n. 14 below). See H. Strathmann, *"leitourgeō,"* in *TDNT,* Vol. 4, pp. 226–31.

13. See Acts 26:5 and Col. 2:18.

fice") and *prosphora* ("offering") occur only with
metaphorical meaning; in the late documents of the
New Testament, however, we can recognize their re-
newed application to worship, to the extent that they
can serve as terms for prayer and praise.[14] The situation is similar with the term *proserchesthai,* "approach" (a deity).[15]

The situation outlined here is not always suffi-
ciently appreciated. The terminological evidence
means not only that any cultic understanding of
Christian worship is out of the question, but also that
there is no longer any distinction in principle between assembly for worship and the service of Christians in the world. Here we clearly find an echo of

14. Most passages containing the word *thysia* refer to the Old
Testament cult: Mark 12:33; Matt. 12:7; Luke 2:24; 13:1; Acts
7:41–42; 1 Cor. 10:18; Hebrews *passim*; likewise the passages containing the word *thysiastērion,* "altar," except for those in Revelation, which refer to the heavenly altar, and Heb. 13:10 (discussed
on p. 86 below). We find christological use of *thysia* in Eph. 5:2;
Heb. 7:27; 9:23–28; 10:12–14, 26; it occurs in parenesis in Rom. 12:1,
and similarly in Phil. 4:18. It is applied to Christian worship in
1 Pet. 2:5, which speaks expressly of *pneumatikai thysiai,* "spiritual
sacrifices," and in Heb. 13:15–16, which, like 12:28, stresses that
"such are the sacrifices which God approves."

On the traditional cultic usage of *anapherein, prospherein* (verbs
meaning "offer") and *prosphora* ("offering"), see Mark 1:44 and
parallels; Matt. 5:23–24; Acts 7:42; 21:26; 24:17; Hebrews
passim; James 2:21. Paul uses *prosphora* in the context of Rom.
15:16 (see n. 12 above). Christological application of this group of
concepts occurs in Eph. 5:2; 1 Pet. 2:24; Heb. 7:27; 9:14, 25, 28;
10:12, 14. The application to prayer occurs in Heb. 5:7 (prayer of
Jesus), to the "sacrifice of praise" in Heb. 13:15, and to "spiritual
sacrifices" in 1 Pet. 2:5.

Hebrews and 1 Peter belong to the subapostolic age; for a discussion of their date, see below, p. 84, n. 23.

15. Apart from a few passages where it is used in the traditional
cultic sense, it, too, occurs only in Heb. 4:16; 7:25; 10:22; 11:6;
12: (18), 22; 1 Pet. 2:4. In Rom. 5:2 and Eph. 2:18; 3:12, which depend on the passage in Romans, *prosagōgē* ("access") is totally removed from the cultic realm.

Jesus' transgression of the boundary between the sacred and the profane. Furthermore, the present eschatological reality does not drive the disciples into seclusion, but calls them forth into the world that God has created and summoned. Thus sacralization has been rendered impossible, and the community of the faithful is established as an open community. Worship in the sense of devotion to God is by no means abolished; but this devotion does not take place in a special defined area, but belongs in the midst of the life lived by Christians. Only thus can Christian worship preserve its essential uniqueness and take on its proper form.

V

The Worship of the
Early Aramaic-Speaking Community

The data concerning the beginnings of Christian worship are not very copious. Unfortunately we are especially poorly informed about the early Aramaic-speaking community of Jerusalem and Palestine. The account furnished by Luke in Acts 2–5 reflects the picture that people at the end of the first century had of the church's origin. To the extent that we are dealing with redactional elements, they have only qualified value as sources. We must therefore inquire into fragments of tradition that have been incorporated in Acts 2–5. Especially illuminating are the Pentecost account and the earliest portions of the so-called résumés or summary accounts (Sammelberichte).[1] This material must be supplemented from the gospels and epistles.[2]

---

1. See above all Ernst Haenchen, *The Acts of the Apostles: A Commentary*, trans. R. McL. Wilson et al. from the 14th German ed. (1965), (Philadelphia: Westminster, 1971), pp. 166–75, 190–96; Martin Dibelius, *Studies in the Acts of the Apostles*, ed. H. Greeven, trans. M. Ling (New York: Scribner's, 1956), especially pp. 1 ff.; H. Zimmermann, "Die Sammelberichte der Apostelgeschichte," *BZ* NF 5 (1961) : 71–82.

2. Gottfried Schille attempts to go his own way methodologically in his *Anfänge der Kirche: Erwägungen zur apostolischen Frühgeschichte*, BEvT 43 (1966) : see also his article "Zur Frage urchristlicher Kultätiologien," *JLH* 10 (1965): 35–54. His theses, in part

The most striking point in the Lukan account is the association of the primitive community with the temple.[3] Does this mean that we must reckon at the outset with marked dependence on Jewish worship? If so, primitive Christian worship would have been constituted in the form of a new synagogal institution associated with the temple cult. Purely externally the primitive community may at first have resembled a special synagogue, but the self-understanding of the community and the nature of their worship preclude such an identification.[4] How, then, are we to define the community's relationship to the temple and to the nomistic tradition of the synagogue? The Aramaic-speaking community probably did not go so far as to reject the temple and law on principle, but the Christians took great liberties with the whole tradition of Old Testament Judaism. This made it possible for them to frame a worship that had central

very problematic, must be subjected to thorough examination, which is impossible in this context; some of his observations are undoubtedly valuable and offer new approaches.

3. This association must be distinguished from the association with Jerusalem, which was occasioned by Jesus' death and certain eschatological expectations associated with the city.

4. Karl Ludwig Schmidt maintains that the term *ekklēsia* goes back to *kᵉništâ* and thus to the designation of a special synagogue; see his "Die Kirche im Urchristentum," in *Festgabe für A. Deissmann* (Tübingen: Mohr, 1927), pp. 258–319; "*ekklēsia,*" in *TDNT,* Vol. 3, pp. 501–36. This theory is misleading in any case. The *ekklēsia*-concept is associated with the idea of the people of God; see L. Rost, *Die Vorstufen von Kirche und Synagoge im Alten Testament,* BWANT 4/24 (1938; reprinted Darmstadt: Wissenschaftliche Buchgesellschaft, 1967); W. G. Kümmel, *Kirchenbegriff und Geschichtsbewusstsein,* Symbolae bibicae upsalienses, 1 (Zurich: Niehaus; Uppsala: Seminarium neotestamenticum upsaliense, 1943), pp. 19 ff.; K. Stendahl, "Kirche im Urchristentum," in *RGG,* Vol. 3, cols. 1297–1304. This conclusion is disputed, in my opinion erroneously, by W. Schrage, "Ekklesia und Synagoge," *ZTK* 60 (1963): 178–202.

importance for the life of the individual and the community. For this reason temple and law lost their preeminent position without being simply negated. Not until later, above all once James the brother of the Lord had taken over sole leadership of the Jerusalem community,[5] did there develop a Jewish Christianity based on strict observance of the law, fidelity to the cult, and a markedly particularistic attitude. An event like that depicted in Acts 21:26, according to which sacrifice was offered by Christians in performance of a vow and as a demonstration of their fidelity to the regulations of the Jewish cult, is probably conceivable only in this period; that Paul himself participated in the sacrificial cult is, despite 1 Corinthians 9:19 ff., most unlikely.[6] Apart from this instance there is no mention of any participation in the sacrificial cult, although in the initial period we should not think in terms of a fundamental decision in this regard. For the primitive community, temple and synagogue were primarily places where they

5. After the initial period under Peter as representative of the twelve, there was a transitional solution to the problem of leadership with the three *styloi* ("pillars") at the head of the community; James the brother of the Lord already had precedence (Gal. 2:9). This probably came about because Peter's missionary activity often took him away from Jerusalem (see Acts 9:31–11:18). After the Apostolic Council and the persecution by Agrippa in 43/44, Peter left Jerusalem entirely (Acts 12:17), and James took over leadership of the community until his martyrdom in A.D. 62 (Josephus, *Antiquities* 20. 200 [20.9.1]).

6. We encounter the same problem in the mention of Timothy's circumcision in Acts 16:3; Gal. 5:11–12 casts grave doubt on the historicity of this tradition. In other cases, too, the value of Acts as a source is somewhat problematical, for instance in its information about the Apostolic Decree (see below, pp. 50–51). For a discussion of 1 Cor. 9:19 ff., see G. Eichholz, "Der missionarische Kanon des Paulus," in his *Tradition und Interpretation*, ThBü 29 (1965), pp. 114–20.

could proclaim the gospel and carry on their mission.[7] When we do read of participation in temple worship, it is in the context of prayer.[8] It is undeniably true that the priests also offered the prescribed sacrifices at the specified times of prayer, but these had lost all their significance for the community. In its polemic citation of Isaiah 56:7, "My house shall be called a house of prayer (for all nations)," Mark 11:17 (and parallels) expresses the specifically Christian understanding of the temple.[9] In other words, the sacrificial cult has lost its meaning, but as long as the temple remains standing it is respected as a place of prayer. There is no other way to understand the development of a Christian worship independent of the temple cult; in any event, it traces its beginnings back to the first post-Easter community.

In this alienation from the sacrificial cult, Jesus' renunciation of temple worship and all cultic and ritual practices probably played a more significant part than we can demonstrate in detail. The independent formation of Christian worship outside a sacral area, on the other hand, is probably more closely linked with the fundamental events of the period immediately after Easter. Jesus' appearances during meals[10] took place, like the Pentecost event, at sites that had no sacral dignity. Therefore primitive Christianity as a whole maintained the principle

7. Acts 3:11 ff.; 5:12 ff. (with the addition of healings); 5:19 ff., 40. "Solomon's Portico," mentioned in Acts 3:11; 5:12, also appears in John 10:23.

8. See Acts 2:46–47; 3:1; also 22:17.

9. For an analysis of this passage see above, pp. 26–30.

10. See Cullmann, *Worship* (cited above, Chap. I, n. 2) , pp. 13 ff.; Rordorf, *Sunday* (cited above, Chap. III, n. 7) , pp. 215 ff.

that worship can no longer take place within well-defined and sanctified precincts. The table fellowships of the disciples and their assemblies *kat' oikon*,[11] at which they continued to experience the presence of the exalted Lord, acquired constitutive significance.[12] The companionship and meals of the earthly Jesus here took on new form; but the Lord's Supper also came to be celebrated with express reference to Jesus' last meal.[13]

Worship *kat' oikon* was characterized, however, not only by table fellowship but in equal measure by the operation of the Spirit. Only so can one explain the significance and function of the prophetic element, which can hardly be overestimated for the earliest period of Christianity. According to the early tradition lying behind Acts 2:1 ff., which was revised and elaborated by Luke,[14] the Pentecost event was

11. There are three different ways of interpreting the phrase *kat' oikon*: (*a*) "in a house," "at home" (preferred by Haenchen, *Acts* [cited above, Chap. V, n. 1], p. 192); (*b*) "by houses" (Goppelt, *Apostolic . . . Times* [cited above, Chap. I, n. 5], p. 45); (*c*) "alternately in their houses," "from house to house" (Cullmann, *Worship* [cited above, Chap. I, n. 2], pp. 9 f. In my opinion the third meaning is out of the question; the first and second are probably not really distinct.

12. This even affected architectural development, so that a special type of "house church" could come into being; see W. Rordorf, "Was wissen wir über den christlichen Gottesdienstraum der vorkonstantinischen Zeit?" *ZNW* 55 (1964) ; 110–28; K. Gamber, *Domus ecclesiae*, Studia patristica et liturgica 2 (Regensburg: Pustet, 1968), especially pp. 63 ff.

13. For a discussion of this point, see my article "Motive" (cited above, Chap. III, n. 17), pp. 338 ff.

14. See K. L. Schmidt, *Pfingstereignis und Pfingsterzählung*, Arbeiten zur Religionsgeschichte des Urchristentums 1/2 (Leipzig: Hinrichs, 1919); N. Adler, *Das erste christliche Pfingstfest*, NTA 18 (1938) ; G. Kretschmar, "Himmelfahrt und Pfingsten," *ZKG* 64 (1954/55): 209–53, especially pp. 234 ff.; Haenchen, *Acts* (cited above, Chap. V, n. 1), pp. 166–75; Hans Conzelmann, *Die Apostelgeschichte*, HNT 7 (1963), pp. 25 ff.

looked upon as a fulfillment of the promise given by the Baptist (Luke 3:16*a,c* and parallel) and indirectly of the Old Testament prophecy in Joel 3. It marks the beginning of the eschatological events involving fire and the Spirit; therefore the eschatological gift of prophecy is also bestowed on the faithful.[15] Prophecy is by no means a phenomenon of the Hellenistic community only; it is also typical of the earliest Christian community. The remarks in Acts 11:27–28; 15:32 expressly mention the names of several prophets from Palestinian communities;[16] Ernst Käsemann's studies of the traditions in the Synoptics, especially Matthew's special material,[17] have removed any doubt that there was already an independent early Christian prophetic movement in the earliest communities. Only on such an assumption can one explain the origin of many logia spoken in the first person with the authority of the exalted Lord, which the community could record without distinguishing them from the pre-Easter words of the Lord.[18] And only on such an assumption can one explain the de-

15. According to the dominant theory of late Judaism, the Spirit had ceased with the last writing prophets; but there were sectarian movements that definitely thought in terms of a continued operation of the Spirit. See R. Meyer and G. Friedrich, *"prophētēs,"* *TDNT*, Vol. 6, pp. 781–861; also my study, *The Titles of Jesus in Christology: Their History in Early Christianity*, trans. H. Knight and G. Ogg (New York & Cleveland: World, 1969), pp. 352-65.

16. The former passage mentions Agabus, the latter Silas and Judas.

17. E. Käsemann, "The Beginnings of Christian Theology," in his *New Testament Questions of Today*, trans. W. J. Montague (Philadelphia: Fortress, 1969), pp. 82–107; idem, "On the Subject of Primitive Christian Apocalyptic," ibid., pp. 108–37. Cf. G. Kretschmar, "Ein Beitrag zur Frage nach dem Ursprung frühchristlicher Askese," *ZTK* 61 (1964) : 27–67, especially p. 38, n. 26.

18. For a different view, see F. Neugebauer, "Geistsprüche und Jesuslogien," *ZNW* 53 (1962) : 218–28.

cidedly charismatic community order of the first period. There is probably no text that better reveals the prophetic awareness of the early community than the logion concerning blasphemy against the Holy Spirit, preserved in its original form in Mark 3:28, while the Q form in Matthew 12:31–32/Luke 12:10 presupposes a division into periods, thus distinguishing the pre-Easter ministry of the Son of man from the final post-Easter salvific operation of the Spirit.[19]

We do not know very much about the details of worship in the earliest community. It assembled "in the name of Jesus."[20] The saying in Matthew 18:20, "Where two or three are assembled in my name, I am there in their midst," is a plain rejection of the Jewish understanding of worship: on the one hand, the presence of the risen Lord replaces the cultic presence of God in the temple; on the other, the requirement of at least ten persons for Jewish worship is abandoned.[21] Baptism with water, borrowed from John the Baptist, was also performed "in the name of Jesus"; it is henceforth associated with the operation of the Spirit.[22] That the Lord's Supper was celebrated

9. For a history of the tradition and its development, see my book *Titles* (cited above, n. 15), pp. 292–93.

20. Correctly determined by W. Hahn, *Gottesdienst* (cited above. Chap. I, n. 2), pp. 89 ff.

21. On Matt. 18:20, cf. the Jewish idea of the *shekinah;* see the discussion by Leipoldt, *Gottesdienst* (cited above, Chap. I, n. 2), p. 18. See also W. C. van Unnik, "Dominus Vobiscum: The Background of a Liturgical Formula," in *New Testament Essays: Studies in Memory of T. W. Manson* (Manchester: Manchester University Press, 1959), pp. 270–305; Wilhelm Pesch, *Matthäus der Seelsorger,* SBib 2 (1966), pp. 43 ff.

22. On the history of baptism in early Christianity we cite merely G. Delling, *Die Taufe im Neuen Testament* (Berlin: Evangelische Verlagsanstalt, 1963), especially pp. 58 ff.

with eschatological rejoicing and passionate expectation of the consummation can be seen clearly from the reference to *agalliasis* ("exultation") and the ejaculation in prayer, *maranatha*.[23] The *anathema* and the admission formula preserved in Didache 10:5, "Whoever is holy, let him approach; whoever is not, let him turn around (be converted)," probably also go back to the early tradition of the Palestinian community. Here we may also mention the invocation of God as "Father," which was characteristic of the community of Jesus' disciples, and the Lord's Prayer. In the context of prayer the liturgical formulas *amēn*, *allēlouia*, and *hōsanna* were borrowed from Judaism, as well as the use of the doxology.[24] Free prayer[25] occupied a preeminent position, but we must also reckon with the likelihood that specific prayer formulas[26] were adopted very early. The initial

23. See R. Bultmann, *"agalliasis,"* in *TDNT*, Vol. 1, pp. 19–21; A. B. du Toit, *Der Aspekt der Freude im urchristlichen Abendmahl* (Winterthur: Keller, 1965), especially pp. 56 ff., 63 ff., 103 ff.; also K. G. Kuhn, *"maranatha,"* in *TDNT*, Vol. 4, pp. 470–73; and my comments in *Titles* (cited above, n. 15), pp. 93 ff.

24. See H. Schlier, *"amēn,"* in *TDNT*, Vol. 1, pp. 335–38; idem, *"allēlouia,"* in *TDNT*, Vol. 1, p. 264; E. Lohse, "Hosianna," *NovT* 6 (1963): 113–19. The *eis aiōna* formula ("for [the] age"; "for ever") in its simple form may probably also be mentioned in this context; see H. Sasse, *"aiōn,"* in *TDNT*, Vol. 1, pp. 197–209.

25. Note the interesting and doubtless very early passage Didache 10:7, according to which a prophet is permitted to give thanks as long as he likes. See also Justin *Apology* 1. 67: *ho proestōs euchas homoiōs kai eucharistias, hosē dynamis autō, anapempei;* "the leader offers up prayers likewise and thanksgivings, as he is able (or, with as much power as he possesses)."

26. Acts 4:24 ff. does not belong in this context; despite the use of several archaic phrases, the text of the prayer is Lukan. See Haenchen, *Acts* (cited above, Chap. V, n. 1), pp. 225–29; Conzelmann, *Apostelgeschichte* (cited above, n. 14), pp. 37–38. *Eulogia* and *eucharistia*, however, were probably already customary in the earliest community. There has never been any doubt that *eulogia*

stages in the framing of creeds,[27] and probably even
the composition of hymnic texts,[28] can likewise be
traced back to this early epoch. The connection with
the Old Testament is obvious, but a new understanding of scripture, and thus a new type of scriptural
interpretation, imposes itself at once.[29] Furthermore,
proclamation of the message of salvation had a fixed

was connected with the Jewish tradition of prayer. Not until the
discovery of the Qumran texts, however, was there evidence that
eucharistia depended on a Jewish formulary; see J. M. Robinson,
"Die Hodajot-Formel in Gebet und Hymnus der Urgemeinde," in
Apophoreta (Haenchen Festschrift), BZNW 30 (1964), pp. 194–235.
For a further discussion of prayer in primitive Christianity, see
Nielen, *Liturgy* (cited above, Chap. I, n. 2), pp. 145 ff.; Delling,
Worship (cited above, Chap. I, n. 2), pp. 104–27; H. Greeven,
Gebet und Eschatologie im Neuen Testament, Neutestamentliche
Forschungen 3/1 (Gütersloh: Bertelsmann, 1931).

27. For a discussion of the beginnings of creeds, see above all
Werner Kramer, *Christ, Lord, Son of God,* trans. B. Hardy, SBT 50
(1966), pp. 13 ff.; from the rest of the copious literature, we men-
tion: O. Cullmann, *The Earliest Christian Confessions,* trans. J. K. S.
Reid (London: Lutterworth, 1949); J. N. D. Kelly, *Early Christian
Creeds* (London: Longmans, 2d ed., 1960); Vernon H. Neufeld,
The Earliest Christian Confessions, New Testament Tools and
Studies 5 (Grand Rapids: Eerdmans, 1963); Martin, *Worship* (cited
above, Chap. I, n. 2), pp. 53 ff.

28. Here we may mention above all the so-called canticles from the
first two chapters of Luke (1:46–55, 68–79; 2:29–32). The *Nunc
Dimittis* in 2:29–32 is the latest text, and occupies a special position.
In the *Magnificat* and *Benedictus* eschatological hymns of Jewish
origin (1:46b, 47, 49–55; 1:68–69, 71–75) have been borrowed and
elaborated from the Christian perspective. See H. Gunkel, "Die
Lieder in der Kindheitsgeschichte Jesu bei Lukas," in *Festgabe
. . . A. von Harnack* (Tübingen: Mohr, 1921), pp. 43–60; E. Klostermann, *Das Lukasevangelium,* HNT 3 (2d ed., 1927), pp. 17 ff., 24 ff.
The situation in Luke 1:76–79 is especially complex: a hymnic text
from the tradition of the Baptist has obviously been borrowed in
verses 76–77, 79b and reinterpreted christologically in verses 78–79a.
See P. Vielhauer, "Das Benedictus des Zacharias," in his *Aufsätze
zum Neuen Testament,* ThBü 31 (1965), pp. 28–46; J. Gnilka, "Der
Hymnus des Zacharias," *BZ* NF 6 (1952): 215–38; and my analysis
in *Titles* (cited above, n. 15), pp. 365 ff. For a general discussion
see also Nielen, *Liturgy* (cited above, Chap. I, n. 2), pp. 282 ff.;
Delling, *Worship* (cited above, Chap. I, n. 2), pp. 91 f.

29. For the earliest period, this new interpretation is most readily
apparent in the passion tradition.

place not only in missionary preaching but also in the worship services of the community. Intimately associated with it, particularly in the assemblies of the community, is the transmission of Jesus' words and the narratives concerning him.[30] It is more difficult to say when "instruction" achieved an independent significance alongside "preaching."[31] In the earliest period there were surely already some readings in the course of worship, as above all the transmission of the passion narrative suggests.[32] The celebration of Sunday, too, probably goes back to the earliest period.[33] An independent early Christian celebration

30. Here we can see clearly the contribution made by form-critical study of the Synoptic traditions to the investigation of early Christian worship. See especially Martin Albertz, *Die Botschaft des Neuen Testaments*, 4 vols. (Zollikon-Zurich: Evangelischer Verlag, 1947-57), Vol. I/1 (1946), Vol. I/2 (1952); and my detailed review in *JLH* 8 (1963) : 86-89.

31. This question provoked the dispute between Dibelius (*Tradition to Gospel* [cited above, Chap. III, n. 13], pp. 9 ff.), who wanted to recognize only "preaching" as the sitz im leben of the gospel tradition, and R. Bultmann (*The History of the Synoptic Tradition*, trans. John Marsh [New York: Harper & Row, 1963], pp. 60-61), who thought from the outset in terms of several sitze im leben. At the start the line between "proclamation" and "instruction" was undoubtedly vague, as can still be seen from Mark's use of *kēryssein* and *didaskein;* only gradually did several clearly distinct stages evolve.

32. In contrast to the independent transmission of the narratives concerning Jesus and of his words, which were only later assembled into larger complexes, the passion narrative was transmitted from the very outset as a single large unit; see Dibelius, *Tradition to Gospel* (cited above, Chap. III, n. 13), pp. 178 ff. The only serious possibilities are its use in catechesis or worship; in my opinion, its establishment in fixed form for the purpose of reading at worship clearly deserves first consideration. A misleading theory has been proposed by G. Schille, "Das Leiden des Herrn," *ZTK* 52 (1955): 161-205, especially pp. 198 ff., according to which definite times for prayer and observances are said to lurk in the background.

33. Clear evidence, however, is not found until 1 Cor. 16:2; Acts 20:7-10; Rev. 1:10; Didache 14:1; and then in Justin *Apology* 1. 67. For a discussion of the individual problems see Rordorf, *Sunday* (cited above, Chap. III, n. 7), pp. 193 ff.

of Passover is also likely.[34] All this may make the basic features of worship apparent in outline, but we cannot make out any specific liturgical order.[35]

Now we must not overlook the fact, already suggested, that there were tendencies at work relatively early among the Jewish Christian communities of Palestine that occasioned a return to ritualism and to Jewish observance of the law. In the Synoptic Gospels this is revealed especially by the question of fasting and observance of the sabbath, in Acts by the problem of circumcision and ritual purity. Following the example of Jesus, the first Christians obviously did not consider themselves bound by Jewish cultic regulations; but they soon subjected this freedom to various limitations. The newly introduced requirement of fasting was based on Jesus' death and bodily departure; at first it may have been only an annual observance, but it became a regular practice, so that later the only difference between Christian and Jewish fasting consisted in the choice of different

34. See H. Schürmann, "Die Anfänge der christlichen Osterfeier," *Theologische Quartelschrift* 131 (1951): 414–25; idem, *Der Paschamahlbericht Lk 22,15–18*, NTA 19/5 (1953), pp. 42–43; A. J. B. Higgins, *The Lord's Supper in the New Testament*, SBT 6 (1952), pp. 47 ff.; my article "Motive" (cited above, Chap. III, n. 17), pp. 352 ff.

35. Acts 2:42 is irrelevant in this context, since it furnishes only a general description of the life of the primitive community; see Ernst Haenchen, *Acts* (cited above, n. 1), p. 189; Conzelmann, *Apostelgeschichte* (cited above, n. 14), p. 31. Jeremias (*Eucharistic Words* [cited above, Chap. III, n. 34], pp. 118 ff.) is of a different opinion; he maintains that we have here a basic order of the earliest form of worship. He takes *koinōnia* in the sense of a fellowship meal (agape), *klasis tou artou* ("the breaking of bread") in the sense of "eucharist," thus drawing a distinction that still cannot be simply assumed for the primitive Christian period; see below, pp. 102–3.

days of the week.[36] Freedom from the sabbath regulations was also originally practiced, but then came to
be considered only a special prerogative of the Son
of man.[37] The disputes, in part severe, concerning
the circumcision of Gentiles and the maintenance of
minimal requirements of ritual purity at table fellowship involving both Jewish and Gentile Christians
led to the Apostolic Council and, in the period of
James the brother of the Lord, to the Apostolic Decree.[38] The appointment of a presbyterate during
the forties was likewise a conscious return to Jewish
practice.[39]

Similar dependence must not be presupposed for
the initial period, as though primitive Christian wor-

36. The primary support for an annual fast is the striking singular
in Mark 2:20b (expressed differently in Matthew and Luke): *en
ekeinē tē hēmera;* see Leipoldt, *Gottesdienst* (cited above, Chap. I,
n. 2), pp. 56–57. Tertullian (*De ieiunio* 2) still mentions an annual
Good Friday fast. Didache 8:1 attests the regular Christian practice
of fasting. See E. Schwartz, *Osterbetrachtungen* (1906), republished
in his *Gesammelte Schriften*, 5 vols. (Berlin: de Gruyter, 1938–63),
Vol. 5 (1963), pp. 1–41, especially pp. 20 ff.; K. Holl, "Ein Bruch-
stück aus einem bisher unbekannten Brief des Epiphanius," in his
Gesammelte Aufsätze zur Kirchengeschichte, 3 vols. (Tübingen:
Mohr, 1928–48), Vol. 2 (1928), pp. 204–24, especially pp. 213–14,
219–20.

37. The saying in Mark 2:27 at the end of the narrative about
plucking grain was expanded by the addition of the christological
declaration in 2:28; Matthew and Luke then limited themselves
to the latter and omitted Mark 2:27.

38. In Acts 15:1–29 (30–33), the Apostolic Council and the requirements of the so-called Apostolic Decree (15:20, 29) are brought together. This is historically inaccurate, as even the statement (deriving from another tradition) in Acts 21:25 shows: according to this
latter passage, James the brother of the Lord does not inform the
Apostle Paul of the requirements contained in the Apostolic Decree until Paul's last visit to Jerusalem. Paul himself never mentions the Decree in Gal. 2:1–10, and never exhibits any knowledge
of it elsewhere or any suggestion that he is bound by it. See my
book *Mission* (cited above, Chap. III, n. 60), pp. 77 ff.

39. See G. Bornkamm, "*presbys, presbyteros,*" in *TDNT*, Vol. 6,
pp. 662–63.

ship were directly related to synagogue worship. Synagogue worship was related to the temple cult, consisted preeminently in legal instruction, and was bound to fixed traditions of prayer; it could therefore hardly have furnished a model for the worship, in the Spirit, of the community assembled in the name of Jesus Christ, no matter how many individual elements were borrowed from synagogal liturgy and employed on a new basis. All in all, we must think in terms of a great range of variations, especially in the earliest period; only gradually did practice tend toward uniformity.

VI

The Worship of
Hellenistic Jewish Christianity

Today there can be no doubt that a Hellenistic Jewish Christianity must be taken into consideration as a connecting link between the primitive Aramaic-speaking community of Palestine and Gentile Christianity. This group played a crucial mediating role.[1] The difference is not primarily geographic but linguistic: according to Acts 6–8, "Hellenists" were already found in Jerusalem. Their most important representatives were Stephen, then Philip and Barnabas. The arrest and stoning of Stephen led to a persecution that befell these very Hellenists.[2] They thereupon began their missionary activity in Samaria, Cyprus, and western Syria; in the metropolis of Antioch on the Orontes they established a new center from which was launched a mission specifically directed toward Gentiles.[3]

1. For more detailed arguments, see my discussion in *Titles* (cited above, Chap. V, n. 15), pp. 12–13, 103 ff., 168 ff., 186 ff., 288 ff., and *passim*.

2. For an analysis of the Stephen tradition, see Johannes Bihler, *Die Stephanusgeschichte im Zusammenhang der Apostelgeschichte*, Münchner theologische Studien 1. (Historische) Abt., Band 16 (Munich: Hüber, 1963); also Martin Scharlemann, *Stephen: A Singular Saint*, AnBib 34 (1968); Marcel Simon, *St. Stephen and the Hellenists in the Primitive Church* (London: Longmans, Green, 1958).

3. See my book *Mission* (cited above, Chap. III, n. 60), pp. 59 ff.

To determine the characteristics of worship in this early Hellenistic Jewish Christianity is almost as difficult as to describe its beginnings in the Aramaic-speaking community. On a few points, however, we can make out the details clearly.

Despite all theological differences and variant traditions,[4] the existence of Jerusalem as the common point of departure must not be ignored.[5] This association with Jerusalem was always maintained by the Antioch group and, despite many tensions, even by Paul. This common origin was fundamental for the unity of early Christianity. We see this clearly in the person of Barnabas: as a "Hellenist" born in Cyprus he belonged to the earliest community when it was still undivided; later he became the leader of the Antioch community, but remained the confidant of the Jerusalemites.[6] The narrative in Acts 6:1–6 re-

4. Worked out precisely but in my opinion overemphasized in U. Wilckens, "Jesusüberlieferung und Christuskerygma—Zwei Wege urchristlicher Überlieferungsgeschichte," *Theologia Viatorum* (*Jahrbuch der Kirchliche Hochschule Berlin*) 10 (1965/66): 310–39.

5. For a different view, see Walter Schmithals, *Paul and James*, trans. D. M. Barton, SBT 46 (1965), pp. 16–37. According to this theory, the "Hellenists" were a group of Jewish Christians dependent on Galilean Christianity, with their home in Syrian Antioch. Not until later did they come to Jerusalem. Acts 11:19 ff. precedes Acts 6–7. Even more radical is the theory of G. Schille, *Anfänge* (cited above, Chap. V, n. 2), pp. 137 ff., 149 ff., 159 ff.: at the outset there was no community at all in Jerusalem, but only in Bethany, Emmaus, and various parts of Galilee (primarily northern). Both Hellenistic Jewish Christian and Palestinian missionaries attempted to gain a foothold in Jerusalem, leading to the martyrdom of Stephen and of James the son of Zebedee. The establishment of the community is associated primarily with Acts 12:3 ff. (and is therefore dated in the forties!); it grew rapidly and achieved a position of preeminence.

6. See Acts 4:36–37; 11:22–26 (also 9:27). The account in Acts 11:22 ff. is not quite accurate, in that it has Barnabas come to Antioch as the envoy of the Jerusalem community; according to 11:25–26, he nevertheless acts as representative of the Antioch community.

veals for the first time that the growth of the primitive community resulted in a kind of grouping into "Hebrews" and "Hellenists." As the linguistic situation made natural, the Hellenistic group had its own communal life, as well as its own charismatic leaders in "the seven." This led understandably to separate development and even a certain amount of dissension; but recognition and commissioning of the seven on the part of the "whole church" provided a solution that satisfied the internal life of primitive Christianity.[7] Opposition to Judaism, however, intensified noticeably, especially on the part of the Hellenists. The eventual result was the persecution of Stephen. The tradition of worship clearly reveals the common origin of both groups. Here we can already speak with good reason of a "liturgical succession."[8] Liturgical formulas, traditions of prayer, confessional statements, etc., were borrowed from the Aramaic-speaking community by Hellenistic Jewish Christian-

In 11:30; 12:25 he is sent as envoy to Jerusalem by the Antioch community, and, according to Acts 15:2, 12, 22, 25; Gal. 2:1, 9, together with Paul represents the Hellenistic community at the Apostolic Council. In 11:22 ff. we can clearly see the special interests of Lukan redaction.

7. Starting with Acts 6, Luke frequently refers to traditions belonging to the Antioch community (though use of an actual source document of Antiochene origin cannot be assumed). The fragment of tradition drawn upon in 6:1–6 is unfortunately unclear in many respects; the tensions can hardly have concerned merely the care of the widows. But the *diakonia kathēmerinē* ("daily distribution," 6:1) probably paved the way for regular cooperation, although surely "the seven," who appear throughout as preachers endowed with the Spirit, did not undertake this table service themselves.

8. The term is used by Franz Rendtorff, *Geschichte des christlichen Gottesdienstes unter dem Gesichtspunkt der liturgischen Erbfolge. Eine Grundlegung der Liturgik*, Studien zur praktischen Theologie 7 (Giessen: Töpelmann, 1914).

ity and then handed on by them.[9] Especially characteristic is the occasional retention of the Hebrew
or Aramaic language.

More significant, of course, are the unique features
of this Hellenistic Jewish Christianity. Of fundamental importance was the very fact that the Old Testament was used, not in the Hebrew original, but in a
Greek version. For the early period, however, we
should not think in terms of a unanimous employ-
ment and recognition of the Septuagint; such use
does not appear until the second half of the first
century, above all in Luke and Hebrews.[10] There
were instead several different Greek versions of the
Old Testament as a whole or of important sections;
these were used in Diaspora Judaism and the earliest
Hellenistic Jewish Christianity.[11] The Greek translation of the Old Testament exerted a profound influence on the ideas and language of preaching, theology,[12] and liturgy. However much the Greek translations sought to preserve specifically biblical ways of
thought, they also bore the stamp of another ideol-

9. Methodologically, we cannot even draw any conclusions about
the primitive Aramaic-speaking community except on the basis of
its tradition as transmitted by the Hellenistic Jewish Christian community.

10. See Traugott Holtz, *Untersuchungen über die alttestamentlichen
Zitate bei Lukas*, TU 104 (1968) ; Friedrich Schröger, *Der Verfasser
des Hebräerbriefs als Schriftausleger*, Biblische Untersuchungen 4
(Regensburg: Pustet, 1968) .

11. For a discussion of these versions, see above all Paul Kahle,
The Cairo Geniza (New York: Praeger, 2d ed. 1959) , pp. 209 ff.;
Krister Stendahl, *The School of St. Matthew*, ASNU 20 (1954) ,
reprinted with new introduction (Philadelphia: Fortress, 1968) ,
pp. 169 ff.

12. See some comments on this influence in my book *Mission*
(cited above, Chap. III, n. 60) , pp. 61 ff.

ogy; this development was not without conse-quences.[13] Now we must also add at once that the thesis maintained by Walter Bauer,[14] according to which one must not simply postulate the use and recitation of the Old Testament in the Hellenistic sphere, is untenable, at least for Hellenistic Jewish Christianity. If we have any useful criterion to dis-tinguish specifically Jewish Christian traditions from Gentile Christian traditions in the Greek-speaking world common to both, it is just this: that Hellenistic Jewish Christianity exhibits a remarkable attach-ment to the intellectual and conceptual world of the Greek Old Testament.[15] But even for Hellenistic Gentile Christianity Bauer's thesis is unlikely: under certain circumstances the Old Testament could be given markedly lower status in these circles, where it probably never achieved the same significance it had for Hellenistic Jewish Christianity; it may never have been used as a whole, but only in the form of sections or extracts; but its presence must be postu-lated everywhere. There is therefore good reason to say that for primitive Christianity as a whole the Old Testament was "the Bible of the church."[16]

13. The Septuagint rendering of Isa. 7:14 is only an especially striking instance *(parthenos* ["virgin"] for *'almá* [Hebrew, "young woman"]) .

14. Walter Bauer, *Der Wortgottesdienst der ältesten Christen* (Tübingen: Mohr, 1930) , now reprinted in his *Aufsätze und kleine Schriften*, ed. G. Strecker (Tübingen: Mohr, 1967) , pp. 155–209, especially pp. 187 ff.; see also Leipoldt, *Gottesdienst* (cited above, Chap. I, n. 2) , pp. 30–31.

15. I have attempted to demonstrate this fact with respect to Christology in my *Titles* (cited above, Chap. V, n. 15) .

16. Hans von Campenhausen, "Das Alte Testament als Bibel der Kirche vom Ausgang des Urchristentums bis zur Entstehung des Neuen Testaments," in his *Aus der Frühzeit des Christentums*

Besides the use of the Greek Old Testament, which in the early period resulted in several less obvious differences and contrasts, there was a much more noticeable difference: a critical attitude toward the law. Even the primitive Aramaic-speaking community was probably lax in observing particular commandments, thanks to Jesus' attitude and their own Spirit-based authority. But this community appears never to have subjected the law itself to fundamental criticism.[17] On this point the Hellenists followed Jesus' intentions much more consistently, questioning the very validity of the law itself.[18] We see this in Acts 6:8 ff., the account of Stephen's trial: he is accused of declaring that Jesus would "change the customs handed down to us by Moses."[19] In Greek terminology, the word *ethē* ("customs," 6:14) refers to the legal regulations of the torah, which have now

(Tübingen: Mohr, 1963), pp. 153–96; see idem, *Die Entstehung der christlichen Bibel*, Beiträge zur historischen Theologie 39 (Tübingen: Mohr, 1968), especially pp. 28 ff. = *The Formation of the Christian Bible*, trans. J. A. Baker, to be published in 1973 by Fortress, Philadelphia).

17. The fragment of tradition incorporated by Luke in Acts 10 is characteristic; see M. Dibelius, "The Conversion of Cornelius," in *Studies* (cited above, Chap. V, n. 1), pp. 109–22.

18. For a different view, see Peter Stuhlmacher, *Das paulinische Evangelium*, Vol. 1, FRLANT 95 (1968), p. 251, n. 2. Stuhlmacher thinks merely in terms of a "pneumatic suspension . . . of the ceremonial law," not a fundamental abrogation of the torah. But the New Testament contains no valid evidence for any distinction between ceremonial and moral law.

19. Acts 6:13–14. That this accusation is made by "false witnesses" does not impugn the accuracy of the charge; as in the trial of Jesus (Mark 14:56 ff.), the accusers are called "false witnesses" because they make the temple saying the basis of a criminal charge. On the formal similarities between the account of Jesus' trial and that of Stephen's trial, see H. W. Surkau, *Martyrien in jüdischer und frühchristlicher Zeit*, FRLANT 36 (1938), pp. 117 ff.

lost their force. The incipient Gentile mission and the immunity from the requirements of circumcision and ritual purity granted the Gentile Christians likewise reveal clearly that we must think in terms of a fundamental abrogation of the law by the Christ-event. As a result, no ritualistic tendencies could appear in this area. The Apostolic Decree was accepted as a formula of compromise only with respect to Jerusalem.[20] A set of regulations for the community after the Jewish pattern was not imposed until much later.[21]

Most important, however, for the worship of the Hellenistic Jewish Christian community was its attitude toward the temple. As the persecution of Stephen shows, there was an explicit renunciation of the Jerusalem temple cult.[22] This is in line with the attitude of this group toward the law; the two are set

20. The Hellenists insisted that the Gentiles converted to the faith were free from the law. But the dispute between Peter and Paul (Gal. 2:11 ff.) led Antioch and Jerusalem to reach an agreement between Jewish and Gentile Christians with respect to table fellowship; four minimum ritual requirements had to be recognized. On the cultic nature of these requirements, see W. G. Kümmel, "Die älteste Form des Aposteldekrets," in his *Heilsgeschehen und Geschichte* (cited above, Chap. III, n. 11), pp. 278–88; Conzelmann, *Apostelgeschichte* (cited above, Chap. V, n. 14), pp. 84–85; K. T. Schäfer, "Aposteldekret," in *Reallexikon für Antike und Christentum* (Stuttgart: Hiersemann), Vol. 1 (1950), cols. 555–58; Schmithals, *Paul and James* (cited above, n. 5), pp. 97 ff. Paul clearly recognized the theological implications of freedom from the law, and drew the appropriate conclusions.

21. See the discussion of James and 1 Peter below, pp. 86–88. The accounts of the appointment of elders in the time of Paul (Acts 14:23; 20:17) are historically inaccurate.

22. The tradition in Acts 6:8–8:3 is not homogeneous. The speech in 7:2–53 is an independent section; the statements about Saul in 7:58b; 8:1a, 3 are also insertions. In the conclusion of the narrative (7:54 ff.) two variant traditions are probably superimposed. See Haenchen, *Acts* (cited above, Chap. V, n. 1), pp. 270–99; Bihler, *Stephanusgeschichte* (cited above, n. 2), pp. 9 ff.

parallel in Acts 6:13–14, and not without reasons. Stephen obviously made reference to Jesus' saying concerning the temple, and among the Hellenists it had its full impact as an attack on the traditional sacrificial cult. While the Hebrews still recognized the temple as God's house and a place of prayer, the Hellenists considered the temple eschatologically superseded. This had far-reaching consequences, for in the traditions of Hellenistic Jewish Christianity we can now discern a comprehensive spiritualization of Jewish cultic ideas. Such spiritualization was also known in the Old Testament and in Intertestamental Judaism, but had never before been linked with an expressly anticultic bias. In the Old Testament, as has recently been elegantly demonstrated,[23] we are not even dealing with a true reinterpretation of the cultic element; the understanding of the cult itself changed, allowing a certain transference of cultic language to noncultic phenomena. At times, of course, this transference was meant to restrain the one-sided priority of the cultic and ritual element.[24] The Qumran community occupies a special position: separation from the Jerusalem cult and the "impious priesthood" of Jerusalem had produced a priestly community leading its own culticly regulated life apart from the temple, with the result that cultic terminology came to be divorced from the worship of the temple. The purpose, however, was far from

23. Hans Jürgen Hermisson, *Sprache und Ritus im alttestament-lichen Kult. Zur "Spiritualisierung" der Kultbegriffe im Alten Testament.* WMANT 19 (1965).

24. See above all Richard Hentschke, *Die Stellung der vorexilischen Schriftpropheten zum Kultus,* BZAW 75 (1957).

being a fundamental criticism of the cult; the ground-work was instead being laid for the restitution of the Jerusalem cult.[25] Criticism of the cult was more apparent in Diaspora Judaism; although emphasis was placed in principle on allegiance to Jerusalem and its temple, various anticultic influences of Hellenism had their effect.[26] This attitude may also have influenced the Hellenistic Jewish Christian community. The decisive factor, however, was the message that the eschaton had dawned, spelling an end to the traditional temple cult. This made possible an unrestricted christological and ecclesiological application of the traditional cultic terminology. The process of spiritualization can be traced especially well with respect to Jesus' saying concerning the temple. Besides the realistic versions, which speak of the end of the earthly temple and the building of an eschatological temple, Mark 14:58 records an ecclesiological reinterpretation. The temple not made by hands, which will be built after three days, is the community constituted by the Easter event. John 2:19 incorporates a christological reinterpretation; while Mark 14:58 still refers back to the earthly temple, even the protasis is spiritualized in John 2:19.[27] In similar fashion, to mention only some especially important passages, we find a christological application of cultic

25. See Bertil Gärtner, *The Temple and the Community in Qumran and the New Testament*, SNTSMS 1 (1965), pp. 4 ff., 16 ff.

26. See Hans Wenschkewitz, *Die Spiritualisierung der Kultusbegriffe Tempel, Priester und Opfer im Neuen Testament*, Angelos Beihefte 4 (Leipzig: Pfeiffer, 1932), pp. 13 ff.

27. In John 2:19 the parallelism is also destroyed in that protasis and apodosis have different subjects: *lysate—egerō* ("[you] destroy this temple . . . , *I* will raise it up").

ideas in 1 Corinthians 5:7 with the Passover lamb, in Romans 3:25 with the *hilastērion*,[28] and in Ephesians 5:2; 1 Peter 1:19 with the idea of sacrifice.[29] In addition, the concept of the temple is used ecclesiologically in 1 Corinthians 3:16; Ephesians 2:19–22; 1 Peter 2:4–5;[30] the idea of sacrifice, as well as that of *logikē latreia*, is so used in Romans 12:1 (–2);[31] and the motif of universal priesthood is so used in 1 Peter 2:9–10 and in Revelation 1:6.[32] Everywhere, whether deliberately or already as a matter of course, rejection of the Old Testament cult is expressed. This interpretation continued to be influential into the period of the Epistle to the Hebrews,[33] the late document

28. It is hardly likely that we should think in terms of the "mercy seat" (*kappōret*) atop the ark, but rather the general Hellenistic concept; see the commentaries *ad loc.*, also P. Stuhlmacher, *Gerechtigkeit Gottes bei Paulus*, FRLANT 87 (1955; 2d ed., 1966), pp. 86 ff.; Karl Kertelge, *"Rechtfertigung" bei Paulus*, NTA NF 3 (1966), pp. 55 ff.

29. Only in these two passages and in Hebrews *passim* is the idea of sacrifice applied to Jesus' death. The interpretation of Jesus' death as being propitiatory ("for us") must not be equated with this notion, since it goes back to a noncultic tradition of atonement; see E. Lohse, *Märtyrer und Gottesknecht*, FRLANT 46 (1955; 2d ed., 1963); also my considerations in "Motive" (cited above, Chap. III, n. 17), pp. 358 ff., especially pp. 362–63.

30. Besides the ecclesiological application of the temple idea in 1 Cor. 3:16, Paul is also familiar with an anthropological application, as 1 Cor. 6:19 shows.

31. See H. Lietzmann, *An die Römer*, HNT 6 (1906; 4th ed., 1933), p. 108; Richard Reitzenstein, *Die Hellenistischen Mysterienreligionen* (Leipzig: Teubner, 1910; 3d ed., 1927; Stuttgart: Teubner, 4th ed., 1956), pp. 328 ff.; O. Casel, "Die *logikē thusia* der antiken Mystik in christlich-liturgischer Umdeutung," in *Jahrbuch für Liturgiewissenschaft* 4 (Münster, 1924): 37–47; Philipp Seidensticker, *Lebendiges Opfer (Röm 12,1)*, NTA 20/1–3 (1954), especially pp. 17 ff., 256 ff.

32. See Wenschkewitz, *Spiritualisierung* (cited above, n. 26), pp. 110 ff. (Paul), 160 ff. (1 Peter).

33. For a discussion of Hebrews, see below, pp. 84–86.

from the Hellenistic Jewish Christian tradition in the New Testament.

There is little to be said here about individual elements in the worship of the Hellenistic Jewish Christian community. In the first place, we are dealing with the data already discussed in the context of the worship of the Aramaic-speaking community; in the second place, much that we still encounter in Paul probably had its roots in the world of Hellenistic Jewish Christianity, although a decision cannot be made with confidence in every instance.[34] Here we shall mention only one especially interesting phenomenon. We learn from the general tradition of Paul and from the Hellenistic Jewish Christianity, above all James and 1 Peter, that there was a so-called standard parenesis incorporating a variety of didactic materials deriving from Diaspora Judaism and Hellenism.[35] Parenesis itself comprises material strung together without real logical or thematic organization. But Christian parenesis probably possesses a fixed framework whose stamp it bears: (a) at the outset it reminds the listeners of their baptism; (b) at its center it has the law of love; and (c) it concludes with eschatological statements.[36] In our context the

---

34. The numerous christological formulas and hymns deserve particular mention. 1 Cor. 15:3-5; Rom. 1:3b-4a; Phil. 2:6-11 surely played an important role in this context.

35. The study of such parenesis has been undertaken especially by Dibelius, *Tradition to Gospel* (cited above, Chap. III, n. 13), pp. 239 ff.; idem, *Der Brief des Jakobus*, KEK 15 (11th ed., 1964, ed. H. Greeven), pp. 13 ff. But see also C. H. Dodd, *Gospel and Law* (New York: Columbia University Press, 1951).

36. Here we cite merely the following sequences: (a) Rom. 12:1-2; James 1:18, 21b (2:7); 1 Peter 1:13 ff., 2:1 ff.; then (b) Rom. 13:8-10; James 2:8-13; 1 Pet. 1:22-23; finally (c) Rom 13:11-14; James 5:7-11; and 1 Pet. 4:7-11.

beginning of the parenesis is especially important. It exhibits not only the postbaptismal character of primitive Christian parenesis, but above all the attempt to forge an intimate bond between the service of Christians in the world and their worship. It is above all in this context, therefore, that spiritualized cultic terms make their appearance.[37] This does not mean that in these parenetic passages we are dealing with liturgical formularies; the materials derive instead from a didactic setting.[38] But what we have already concluded from our discussion of terminology is confirmed: the boundary between worship and the world remains fluid; there is no Christian worship without responsibility for one's fellowman.

Thus Hellenistic Jewish Christianity arrived at an understanding of Christian worship free of all dependence on the law and the temple and consequently including the total life of the community and of the individual Christians. The transferred application of cultic terminology played a significant role in the process.

37. Rom. 12:1*b*; James 1:26–27; 1 Pet. 1:16, 18–19; 2:5, 9–10.
38. The parenetic material in Paul and James exhibits no liturgical stylization. The situation is different in Colossians and Ephesians, but also in 1 Peter.

VII

The Worship of
Early Gentile Christianity

In 1 Corinthians we confront early Gentile Christianity and its problems in full force.[1] But it is certainly not true that the situation we encounter there is unique and that we cannot make generalizations about it. The important thing is to distinguish between the elements of worship adopted by the Corinthians and the special circumstances of the local community. The specifically Corinthian problem is the unrestricted practice of supposedly Christian freedom,[2] revealing itself in worship primarily in the totally one-sided dominance of ecstatic phenomena. For the rest, however, it is evident that we must presuppose the same fundamental motifs of worship as are found elsewhere. Paul emphasizes the authoritative nature of these motifs, and for his own part appeals to the consensus of the "communities of God."[3]

1. See primarily 1 Corinthians 8–10; 11; 12–14.
2. Even in the realm of sexual ethics, as 1 Cor. 6:12–20 shows; cf. also 1 Cor. 5:1 ff.
3. Apart from 1 Cor. 4:17; 7:17b; 11:16 (for a discussion of 14:33b see below, n. 40), we refer to the authoritative form of the Lord's Supper tradition (11:23–25[26]) and of the christological kerygma (15:3–5).

It is instructive that expressions resembling confessional statements in their wording have a clear priority in the first Gentile Christian communities. In 1 Corinthians 8:4, 6 we meet for the first time a two-part confessional formula whose first line derives unmistakably from the Shema.[4] This confession determines the relationship between the Christian community and its pagan environment, especially with respect to the pagan cult. The question already arises with respect to meat offered to idols: in the ancient world, the slaughtering of animals for food was almost always a ritual act. Such meat may be purchased and eaten; in this matter Christian freedom is at all events appropriate. But the situation is different with respect to sacrificial meals. Paul does agree with the "strong" that in principle it should even be possible to participate in a sacrificial meal at the *eidōleion* ("idol's temple," 8:10); but concern for the "weak" and edification of the community set a limit that cannot be transgressed, for " 'all things are lawful,' but not all things build up [the community]."[5] According to 1 Corinthians 12:2–3, the content of the Christian confession distinguishes the operation of the Spirit in the Christian community from all outwardly comparable ecstatic phenomena of the pagan cults.[6]

4. See Cullmann, *Confessions* (cited above, Chap. V, n. 27), pp. 21 f., 42, 46.

5. 1 Cor. 10:23. The situation differs somewhat in Rom. 14:1 ff.; but Paul immediately associates the problems of asceticism with the fundamental considerations in 1 Corinthians 8–10.

6. Here we should probably not think in terms of gnostic rejection of the earthly Jesus, as suggested by W. Schmithals, *Gnosticism in Corinth*, trans. John E. Steely (Nashville: Abingdon, 1971), pp. 124 ff. A similar view is espoused by E. Güttgemanns, *Der leidende Apostel und sein Herr*, FRLANT 90 (1966), pp. 62 ff. The counter-argument is rightly presented by Dieter Lührmann, *Das Offen-*

At Corinth the operation of the Spirit made a powerful and vital impression; "distinguishing between spirits" was seen to be all the more necessary.[7] Intimately associated was the question of special gifts of the Spirit or charismata.[8] In 1 Corinthians 12:28 Paul provides a list that must at least in its original form be pre-Pauline. In contrast to Romans 12:6 ff., he is also not concerned to include the humble forms of serving and to characterize them as charismata; but in 1 Corinthians 12:4–27 he is concerned to stress the unity of spiritual gifts as well as their diversity.[9] For this purpose he draws on the notion of the body of Christ, which he supplements with the idea of a biological organism.[10] On the basis of these fundamental considerations, he speaks in chapter 13 of *agapē* as the way superior to all charismata, to be sought and

barungsverständnis bei Paulus und in den paulinischen Gemeinden, WMANT 16 (1965), pp. 28–29. See also the discussion between K. Maly, "1 Kor 12,1–3, eine Regel zur Unterscheidung der Geister?" BZ NF 10 (1966) : 82–95, and N. Brox, "ΑΝΑΘΗΜΑ ΙΗΣΟΥΣ (1 Kor 12,3)," BZ NF 12 (1968) : 103–11.

7. See 1 Cor. 12:10; 1 Thess. 5:20–21; 1 John 4:1; and the especially interesting passage Didache 11:2, 5–6, 7 ff.

8. In 1 Cor. 12:1, we are probably not dealing with the masculine form *pneumatikoi* ("spiritual men") but with the neuter *pneumatika* ("spiritual gifts"), parallel to *charismata* in 12:4. For a discussion of the Pauline understanding of spiritual gifts, see H. Greeven, "Propheten, Lehrer, Vorsteher bei Paulus," ZNW 44 (1952/53) : 1–43; Hans von Campenhausen, *Ecclesiastical Authority and Spiritual Power in the Church of the First Three Centuries*, trans. J. A. Baker (Stanford: Stanford University Press, 1969), pp. 55 ff., 60 ff.; G. Ruhbach, "Das Charismaverständis des Neuen Testaments," *Monatsschrift für Pastoraltheologie* 53 (1964) : 407–19.

9. The dominant idea is that gifts of the Spirit obligate their recipients to serve; this is why *diakonia* (ministering) is stressed. See Eduard Schweizer, *Church Order in the New Testament*, trans. F. Clarke, SBT 32 (1961), pp. 89 ff., 157 ff.; E. Käsemann, "Ministry and Community in the New Testament," in his *Essays* (cited above, Chap. III, n. 8), pp. 63–94.

10. For an interpretation of the notion of the body of Christ, see E. Schweizer, "*sōma*," in *TDNT*, Vol. 7, pp. 1067 ff. (bibliography).

followed by every Christian.[11] In chapter 14 he then comes to the problems of worship. The dominant notion is edification of the community, to which programmatic reference has already been made in 1 Corinthians 8:1, 10 and 10:23.[12]

1 Corinthians 14 is the only text in the New Testament that takes a position with respect to Christian worship. Apart from the primary problem of speaking in tongues, several elements of worship also encountered elsewhere are cited in Paul's exposition. Especially productive are 14:6 (*apokalypsis, gnōsis, prophēteia, didachē;* "revelation, knowledge, prophecy, teaching") and 14:26 (*psalmos, didachē, apokalypsis, glōssa, hermēneia;* RSV, "hymn, lesson, revelation, tongue, interpretation"); in addition, according to 14:13 ff., we have *eucharistein* ("give thanks") and *eulogein* ("bless") as well as the response *amēn* on the part of the community; finally, we may add *sophia,* "wisdom" (or *logos sophias,* "utterance of wisdom," alongside *logos gnōseōs,* "utterance of knowledge") and *diakrisis pneumatōn* ("the ability to distinguish between spirits") from 1 Corinthians 12:8, 10, and *maranatha* ("our Lord, come!") from 16:22. Despite some overlapping, we find here hymns and prayers followed by "Amen"; then proclamation of the word in various forms;[13] and speaking in

11. On the transition in 1 Cor. 12:31, see G. Iber, "Zum Verständnis von 1 Cor 12:31," *ZNW* 54 (1963) : 43–52; on 1 Corinthians 13, see Günther Bornkamm, "The More Excellent Way (I Corinthians 13) ," in his *Early Christian Experience,* trans. Paul L. Hammer (New York: Harper & Row, 1969) , pp. 180–93.

12. See G. Bornkamm, *Paul,* trans. D. M. G. Stalker (New York: Harper & Row, 1971) , pp. 186 ff.

13. These include prophecy, instruction, revelation, words of wisdom, and words of knowledge.

tongues together with translation, while the gift of *diakrisis pneumatōn* ("distinguishing among spirits") is assigned a superior function. With one exception, all these elements of worship can also be found outside 1 Corinthians, and even *logos gnōseōs* ("utterance of knowledge") probably existed previously. The meaning of *psalmos* can easily be visualized on the basis of the earliest christological hymns.[14] *Eulogia* and *eucharistia* are also familiar to us from their use in the proemia or thanksgivings of the New Testament letters.[15] The prayer formulas *amēn* and *maranatha*[16] speak for themselves. The situation is

14. See especially Phil. 2:6–11. For a discussion of this passage, see above all Ernst Lohmeyer, *Kyrios Jesus* (Heidelberg: Winter, 1928, reprinted 1961); idem, *Der Brief an die Philipper*, KEK 9/1 (12th ed., 1961), pp. 90 ff., and the supplement by W. Schmauch, KEK 9 (13th ed., 1964), pp. 21 ff.; E. Käsemann, "Kritische Analyse von Phil 2,5–11," in his *Exegetische Versuche und Besinnungen*, 2 vols. (Göttingen: Vandenhoeck & Ruprecht, 1960–64), Vol. 1 (1960), pp. 51–95; E. Schweizer, *Lordship and Discipleship*, SBT 28 (1960), pp. 61 ff.; Ralph P. Martin, *Carmen Christi. Philippians ii. 5–11 in Recent Interpretation and in the Setting of Early Christian Worship*, SNTSMS 4 (1967); Joachim Gnilka, *Der Philipperbrief*, HTKNT 10/3 (1968), pp. 111 ff., 131 ff.; also R. Deichgräber, *Gotteshymnus und Christushymnus in der frühen Christenheit*, Studien zur Umwelt des Neuen Testaments 5 (Göttingen: Vandenhoeck & Ruprecht, 1967), pp. 118 ff., a fundamental book for the analysis of the New Testament hymns. The study by G. Schille, *Urchristliche Hymnen* (Munich: Kaiser, 1962), is not convincing either in its definition of the literary type or in its examination of the individual texts. See most recently Jack T. Sanders, *The New Testament Christological Hymns: Their Historical Religious Background*, SNTSMS 15 (1971), pp. 9–12, 58–74.

15. *Eulogia* is found in 2 Cor. 1:3–11; Eph. 1:3–14; 1 Pet. 1:3–12; *eucharistia* occurs in Rom. 1:8–17; 1 Cor. 1:4–9; Phil. 1:3–11; 1 Thess. 1:2–10; also 2 Thess. 1:3–12; Col. 1:9–20, as well as Eph. 1:15–23 and elsewhere. See above, Chap. V, n. 26.

16. The phrase *abba ho patēr* ("Abba! Father!"; Gal. 4:6 and Rom. 8:15) also deserves mention here. In the New Testament we are usually dealing with a prayer addressed to God. For prayer addressed to Christ (besides *maranatha*) see Acts 7:59 and 2 Cor. 12:8–9, apart from the homology *epikaleisthai to onoma Iēsou* ("to call on the name of Jesus"). Prayer is usually made "in the name of Jesus (Christ)" or "through (Jesus) Christ"; see Nielen, *Liturgy*

more difficult with respect to the various forms of proclamation of the word,[17] which cannot be clearly distinguished. In addition, certain displacements in content have already taken place, as the criticism of *prophēteia* in 1 Corinthians 14 reveals. *Didachē* occupies a relatively clear and independent place; it is considered an especially important charismatic gift both in pre-Pauline tradition and by Paul himself.[18] *Logos sophias* and most likely also *logos gnōseōs* are probably associated with insight into God's plan and will for salvation,[19] *apokalypsis* with declaration of God's concrete purpose for the present or future.[20] Even before Paul *prophēteia* signifies the proclamation of salvation through the operation of the Spirit, but largely in association with ecstatic glossolalia; Paul emphasizes instead the lucidity and rationality of the prophetic message,[21] taking into account the

(cited above, Chap. I, n. 2) , pp. 222 ff., 163 ff.; A. Oepke, *"dia,"* in *TDNT*, Vol. 2, pp. 65–70, especially pp. 68–69; my book *Titles* (cited above, Chap. V, n. 15) , p. 376, with n. 172; Wilhelm Thüsing, *Per Christum in Deum*, NTA NF 1 (1965; 2d ed., 1968) , pp. 165 ff., especially pp. 174 ff.; Moule, *Worship* (cited above, Chap. I, n. 2) , pp. 70 ff. See also Günther Harder, *Paulus und das Gebet*, NTA 4/10 (1936) .

17. For a summary of the discussion, see Delling, *Worship* (cited above, Chap. I, n. 2) , pp. 92 ff.; R. Asting, *Die Verkündigung des Wortes im Urchristentum* (Stuttgart: Kohlhammer, 1939) ; Martin, *Worship* (cited above, Chap. I, n. 2) , pp. 66 ff.

18. For a discussion of *didachē* as a charisma, see Greeven, "Propheten" (cited above, n. 8) , pp. 16 ff. On the function and significance of instruction in primitive Christianity, see Nielen, *Liturgy* (cited above, Chap. I, n. 2) , pp. 251–62; K. H. Rengstorf, *"didaskō,"* in *TDNT*, Vol. 2, pp. 135–48.

19. See on the one hand 1 Cor. 1:21, 30; 2:6 ff., on the other 1 Cor. 13:2, 8; 2 Cor. 2:14; 4:6; and *passim*.

20. See Gal. 2:2 and Rom. 11:25 ff. *(mystērion)* .

21. See the important study by Günther Bornkamm, "Faith and Reason in Paul," in his *Experience* (cited above, n. 11) , pp. 29–46, especially pp. 38 ff. See also Nielen, *Liturgy* (cited above, Chap. I, n. 2) , pp. 268 ff.; G Friedrich, *"prophētēs,"* in *TDNT*,

goal of converting the *idiōtai* and *apistoi* (RSV, "outsiders and unbelievers").[22] Thus prophecy, alongside apostolic preaching, is the form most markedly missionary in intent. Apart from the now necessary restriction of ecstatic phenomena, 1 Corinthians 14 reveals an astounding variety in the conduct of worship.[23] There is no official supervision of details or adherence to a fixed liturgical order which would suppress any free expression of the Spirit; Paul nevertheless assumes that everything is done *kata taxin* ("in order," 14:40), and himself gives instructions in this regard.[24] To the mind of primitive Christianity, the Spirit and order are no more mutually exclusive than are the Spirit and (church) law (Recht); but order and law, to the extent that they are determined

Vol. 6, pp. 856 ff. My assistant H. Paulsen points out that even before Paul prophecy was separate from glossolalia, and that elsewhere, too, prophecy is usually intelligible (Agabus; the seven letters in Revelation). Paul was nevertheless the first to demand a clear distinction, definitely characterizing prophecy as being lucid and assigning to glossolalia a special function and subordinate status.

22. 1 Cor. 14:23–25. Here *idiōtai* refers to individuals on the fringe of the congregation, corresponding to the Jewish *phoboumenoi* or *sebomenoi ton theon* ("God-fearers," "worshipers of God"), who are sympathetic to the community but have not yet joined it. In this context also we hear for the first time of liturgical obeisance (*proskynēsis*). Heavenly obeisance is mentioned in Phil. 2:10 (cf. Heb. 1:6; Revelation *passim*). For a discussion of "outsiders," see *A Greek-English Lexicon of the New Testament and Other Early Christian Literature*, by Walter Bauer, trans. and adapted from the 4th German ed. (1952) by W. F. Arndt and F. W. Gingrich (Chicago: University of Chicago Press, 1957), "*idiōtēs*," p. 371; in the 5th German ed. (1958), pp. 732–33; idem, "Mündige und Unmündige bei dem Apostel Paulus," reprinted in his *Aufsätze* (cited above, Chap. VI, n. 14), pp. 122–54, especially pp. 152 ff.; H. Schlier, "*idiōtēs*," in *TDNT*, Vol. 3, pp. 215–17.

23. Most of the elements whose presence can be demonstrated in Gentile Christianity probably derive in turn from Hellenistic Jewish Christianity, in which their presence can likewise be assumed.

24. 1 Cor. 14:26–33*a*, 36–40.

by the operation of the Spirit, cannot be institution-alized and codified, certainly not in the context of the community assembled for worship.[25]

The information we glean from 1 Corinthians 14 is deficient in two respects. In the first place, there is no mention of any reading of scripture; but even apart from individual quotations, we may assume familiarity with and regular use of scripture on the basis of the typological argument in 1 Corinthians 10:1 ff. and the midrash in 2 Corinthians 3:4 ff.[26] In the second place, 1 Corinthians 14 does not mention the Lord's Supper; as 1 Corinthians 11:17 ff. shows, it was naturally in use, but comparison of 1 Corinthians 11:17 ff. and 1 Corinthians 14 shows that the "unified worship"[27] repeatedly assumed to have ex-isted throughout primitive Christianity is not very likely. The separate existence of a worship service consisting of word of God and prayer can hardly be disputed.[28]

When we turn to the problems peculiar to Corinth, besides the abuses at the celebration of the Lord's

25. The antithesis between the Spirit and church law has been represented above all by Rudolf Sohm, *Kirchenrecht*, 2 vols. (Munich: Duncker & Humblot, 1892–1923), Vol. 1 (1892); see D. Stoodt, *Wort und Recht: Rudolf Sohm und das theologische Problem des Kirchenrechts* (Munich: Kaiser, 1962), especially pp. 38 ff., 70 ff., where he makes the point that one must note both the juridical nature of acclamation in the Spirit and of the sacra-ment, as well as the function of "holy law" (see below, n. 50).

26. This holds true even more for Galatians and Romans: in Galatia, as at Rome, we must think in terms of a significant per-centage of Gentile Christians.

27. Above all in Cullmann, *Worship* (cited above, Chap. I, n. 2), pp. 26 ff. For a discussion, see Goppelt, *Apostolic . . . Times* (cited above, Chap. I, n. 5), pp. 210–12.

28. Bauer, *Wortgottesdienst* (cited above, Chap. VI, n. 14), as re-printed in his *Aufsätze*, pp. 155 ff.

Supper deriving from a marked tendency to sacramentalize,[29] we find above all that Paul considered the dominance of ecstatic manifestations questionable. At Corinth glossolalia was considered an especially noteworthy charisma. Paul does not reject speaking in tongues, but restricts its scope: it has its place in private prayer, but it belongs in corporate worship only when there is someone to translate its meaning.[30] For Paul, this emphasis on lucid speech and demand that prophecy be given precedence is associated with the missionary function of all worship.[31] Just as there is no place for any ritual or cultic demarcation of a special area set aside for worship, so too there is no place for any sectarian introversion of the devout, such as contemporary paganism had in plenty in the form of the mystery cults and their devotees.

The worship of the community must not only be open to the outside world, it must also extend beyond assembly for worship in the narrow sense. Paul made this point emphatically in Romans 12, a chapter that has well been given the title "Service of God in the Everyday Life of the World."[32]

29. This can be seen clearly in 1 Cor. 10:1 ff.; 11:17 ff.; for a detailed discussion, see G. Bornkamm, "Lord's Supper and Church in Paul," in his *Experience* (cited above, Chap. VII, n. 11), pp. 123–60, especially pp. 126 ff.; Paul Neuenzeit, *Das Herrenmahl*, StANT 1 (1960), pp. 26 ff.

30. See Nielen, *Liturgy* (cited above, Chap. I, n. 2), pp. 273 ff.; Delling, *Worship* (cited above, Chap. I, n. 2), pp. 32 ff.; F. W. Beare, "Speaking with Tongues," *Journal of Biblical Literature* 83 (1964): 229–46.

31. We must probably also assume that the Lord's Supper had a missionary function; cf. 1 Cor. 16:22 and Didache 10:6.

32. E. Käsemann, "Worship in Everyday Life: a note on Romans 12," in his *Questions* (cited above, Chap. V, n. 17), pp. 188–95. On the missionary function of the church, see E. Schweizer, "The

Finally, a most interesting theme appears in 1 Corinthians 11:2–16: the role of women in worship. They are not forbidden to pray or prophesy (in other words, to proclaim the word) in the assembled congregation; their right to do so is expressly recognized. On this point the reference to what other congregations do is especially informative.[33] The statements about Prisca (Priscilla) reveal furthermore that in the Hellenistic Jewish Christian communities women already were accorded a substantially more independent role and that they could be assigned a special function in worship on the basis of a charisma.[34] This is assumed and practiced at Corinth. A problem arose on another point, however, when the idea of freedom clearly led to a general emancipation of women, an emancipation that no longer had anything to do with the freedom of the children of God and their particular gifts of grace.[35] It is a necessary reali-

---

Church as Missionary Body of Christ," in his *Neotestamentica* (Zurich: Zwingli, 1963), pp. 317–29; G. Eichholz, "Der ökumenische und missionarische Horizont der Kirche," in his *Tradition* (cited above, Chap. V, n. 6), pp. 85–98.

33. 1 Cor. 11:16.

34. For Prisca, see 1 Cor. 16:19; Rom. 16:3; Acts 18:2, 18, 26; especially interesting is her precedence over Aquila in Rom. 16:3 and Acts 18:18, 26. Even Jezebel (Rev. 2:20) is attacked only for her false teaching. Montanism is also familiar with women who prophesy. This may go back to the influence of the prophecy in Joel 2:28–29, "your sons *and your daughters* will prophesy, . . . menservants *and maidservants*" (suggested by H. Paulsen). A liturgical function for women is strictly ruled out by the regulations governing the synagogue.

35. It is incorrect, however, to describe the situation in the terms of Ernst von Dobschütz, *Christian Life in the Primitive Church*, trans. G. Bremen (London: Williams & Norgate, 1904), p. 37. According to him, we are dealing with abuses for which "emancipated women must have played an important part . . . evidently the least trustworthy element in the Church, the soul of the opposition against the Apostle and his earnest discipline."

zation for Paul that before God all are equally sinners in need of justification; it is clear to him that all the baptized are equal in the body of Christ.[36] But this equality does not abolish differences in the creaturely realm and with respect to gifts of grace.[37] The wearing of a veil as discussed in 1 Corinthians 11:2 ff. is an incidental motif of secondary importance; its importance for Paul is only symbolic, as representing a much more fundamental situation. The crucial point, alongside the statements of equality, which are maintained with full force, is for Paul the particular position of women, a position here grounded on christological arguments.[38] Only when this is taken into account and liturgical functions are accorded women solely on the basis of a special charisma is appropriate participation possible. It has already been suggested[39] that in 1 Corinthians 11 we see a retrograde development with respect to the participation of women in worship; this position cannot be maintained. But it remains true that the argument brought forward by Paul in 11:3, taken out of context, could be developed along the lines of an "order of creation" to preclude all participation of women in worship. This can be seen in the intimately

---

36. Cf. Rom. 3:9, 23 ff.; Gal. 3:26 ff.; likewise 1 Cor. 11:11–12.

37. Most illuminating is the way the question of slavery is treated in 1 Cor. 7:17 ff. and Philemon. According to Adolf Schlatter, *Gottes Gerechtigkeit* (Stuttgart: Calwer, 2d ed., 1952), pp. 336–37, in Rom. 12:3 ff. also Paul is resisting the "seductive power of the ideal of equality."

38. 1 Cor. 11:3, ". . . the head of every man is Christ, the head of a woman is her husband, and the head of Christ is God."

39. Nielen, *Liturgy* (cited above, Chap. I, n. 2), pp. 355 ff.

related passages at 1 Corinthians 14:34–35 and 1 Timothy 2:11 ff. The much-disputed passage about women keeping silent (1 Cor. 14:34–35), the exact place of which is obscure on textual grounds and which moreover interrupts the train of thought in 14:32–33 and 36 ff., cannot derive from Paul, as comparison with 1 Corinthians 11:2–16 shows on the basis of contents.[40] In deutero-Pauline circles this position was maintained in the face of the apostle's own attitude. First Timothy 2:11–15 hearkens back quite deliberately to Jewish ideas.[41] The fact that these statements also occur in the New Testament does not relieve us of the decision whether such a Judaizing tendency within the early Christian church was legitimate.

Apart from the detailed discussions of baptism and the Lord's Supper,[42] we find in Paul a whole series of liturgical traditions. Here belong above all the greetings in the introductory sections of the letters,[43] and the concluding sections which are strongly influenced by features in preparation for the Lord's Sup-

40. This point is discussed in detail, in light of the current literature, by G. Fitzer, *"Das Weib schweige in der Gemeinde."* Über den upaulinischen Charakter der mulier-taceat-Verse in 1 Kor 14, Theologische Existenz heute NF 110 (Munich: Kaiser, 1963). See also J. Leipoldt, *Die Frau in der antiken Welt und im Urchristentum* (Leipzig: Koehler, 2d ed., 1955), pp. 170 ff., especially pp. 187 ff.; for a different view, see Else Kähler, *Die Frau in den paulinischen Briefen* (Zurich: Gotthelf, 1960), pp. 70 ff.

41. See the commentaries; a similar view is found in 1 Pet. 3:1–6.

42. See Gal. 3:26 ff.; Rom. 6:3 ff.; 1 Cor. 10:1 ff., 16 ff.; 11:17 ff.

43. These are accurately described by E. Lohmeyer, "Briefliche Grussüberschriften," in his *Probleme paulinischer Theologie* (Stuttgart: Kohlhammer, 1954), pp. 3–29; for a different approach, see G. Friedrich, "Lohmeyers These über das paulinische Briefpräskript kritisch beleuchtet," *TLZ* 81 (1956): 343–46.

per,[44] including a holy kiss[45] and a special formula
of blessing.[46] Alongside the various forms of blessing[47]
we also encounter curses in Paul, not only in the form
of the anathema at the Lord's Supper,[48] but also in
place of a proemium in Galatians 1:6 ff. and in the
context of the liturgical act of handing over a sinner
to Satan in 1 Corinthians 5:1 ff.[49] In 1 Corinthians
5:1 ff., as in 16:22, the anathema occurs in instructive association with holy law.[50] Just as Paul resists
all Judaizing, he also passionately attacks all syn-
cretistic and ascetic efforts.[51] Whether the Jewish
Passover and Pentecost festivals continued to be celebrated in Christianized form by the Pauline com-

44. See the illuminating discussion by G. Bornkamm, "Das
Anathema in der urchristlichen Abendmahlsliturgie," *TLZ* 80
(1950) : cols. 227 ff., reprinted in his *Das Ende des Gesetzes,* BEvT
16 (= his *Gesammelte Aufsätze* Band 1; 4th ed., 1965) , pp. 123–32.

45. See Reinhold Seeberg, "Kuss und Kanon," in his *Aus Religion
und Geschichte (Gesammelte Aufsätze)* (Leipzig: Deichert, 1906),
pp. 118–22; K. M. Hofmann, *Philema hagion,* BFChrTh 2/38
(1938) .

46. Even including the triadic formula 2 Cor. 13:14.

47. See Friedrich Horst, "Segen und Segenshandlungen in der
Bibel," in his *Gottes Recht,* ThBü 12 (1961) , pp. 188–202; idem.
"Segen," in *RGG,* Vol. 5, cols. 1649–51; Lyder Brun, *Segen und
Fluch im Urchristentum* (Olso: Bybwad, 1932) ; W. Schenk, *Der
Segen im Neuen Testament,* Theologische Arbeiten, 25 (Berlin:
Evangelische Verlagsanstalt, 1967) ; Claus Westermann, *Der Segen in
der Bibel und im Handeln der Kirche* (Munich: Kaiser, 1968) ,
especially pp. 66 ff.

48. The traditional formula occurs in 1 Cor. 16:22; in 1 Cor. 11:27
ff. Paul develops the tradition independently.

49. On this text, certain details of which present great difficulties,
see the commentaries, especially J. Weiss, *Der erste Korintherbrief,*
KEK 5 (9th ed., 1910) , pp. 123 ff.; H. Conzelmann, *Der erste
Korintherbrief,* KEK 5 (11th ed., 1969) , pp. 114 ff.

50. See E. Käsemann, "Sentences of Holy Law in the New Testament," in his *Questions* (cited above, Chap. V, n. 17) , pp. 66–81.

51. See on the one hand Gal. 4:9 ff., on the other Rom. 14:1 ff.

munities is hard to determine.[52] But Paul definitely assumes that Sunday was celebrated as a matter of course.[53]

Gentile Christianity of the apostolic period borrowed significant elements from Hellenistic Jewish Christian worship. The operation of the Spirit plays an especially important role. But differentiation is necessary from the paganism of the past and of the surrounding world with respect to both idolatry (hence the formation of a two-part confession) and misunderstood ecstasy and abuse of freedom. Paul deals with these problems without restricting the abundance and variety of liturgical practice; but he does require that spirits be tested and that everything done be judged by the standard of missionary mandate and of the edification of the church.

52. See Acts 20:6 and 1 Cor. 16:8.
53. In 1 Cor. 16:1–2 for Galatia and Corinth.

VIII

The Worship of
the Subapostolic Period

In the subapostolic period[1] many changes took place that affected the understanding and form of worship. Most of the New Testament documents came into being in this period; but there is little direct information about worship, and we are largely dependent on indirect conclusions. Much more, however, can be derived from the extant texts than is usually realized.

The Revelation of John is always taken into consideration, but often interpreted inappropriately. This book, which came into being during the Domitianic persecution in A.D. 95/96, is interesting because in connection with the reception of apocalyptic Jewish material it records very early Jewish Christian traditions, obviously of Palestinian provenance.[2] Apart

1. The subapostolic period is understood as the epoch from the death of Paul, Peter, and James the brother of the Lord at the beginning of the sixties to the turn of the century.

2. Palestinian Jewish Christians probably emigrated after the catastrophe of the Jewish War and thus arrived in Asia Minor. The seven communities mentioned in Revelation 2 and 3 were probably the most important centers of resettlement; the Jewish Christians probably formed their own congregations alongside the existing Christian communities.

from certain eschatological and christological views,[3] this background appears especially in ecclesiastical organization.[4] The communities presupposed here still have prophets as official functionaries.[5] There is no trace of anything comparable either in the Jerusalem community under James the brother of the Lord or in the contemporary communities of Asia Minor; a "Jewish Christian conventicle"[6] is probably in the background. We should therefore assume a worship tradition essentially bearing the stamp of Jewish Christianity. Numerous liturgical elements and constituents are in fact discernible. But it would be erroneous simply to interpret the statements about heavenly worship as reflecting the earthly worship services of this community.[7] Neither is it appropriate to attempt to demonstrate that the entire book exhibits a "liturgical structure."[8] The author makes use of the epistolary schema and the forms of prophecy and revelation; on a small scale he frequently employs predications, doxologies, acclamations, and

3. See Traugott Holtz, *Die Christologie der Apokalypse des Johannes*, TU 85 (1962).

4. See Akira Satake, *Die Gemeindeordnung in der Johannesapokalypse*, WMANT 21 (1966).

5. G. Bornkamm, "*presbyteros*," in *TDNT*, Vol. 6, pp. 668–70; Satake, *Gemeindeordnung* (cited above, n. 4), pp. 47 ff., 155 ff.

6. Satake, *Gemeindeordnung* (cited above, n. 4), pp. 1 ff., 194–95. But see the critical review by T. Holtz in *TLZ* 93 (1968): 262–64.

7. This approach is taken by Leipoldt, *Gottesdienst* (cited above, Chap. I, n. 2), pp. 44, 47–48; Eduard Lohse, *Die Offenbarung des Johannes*, Das Neue Testament Deutsch 11 (Göttingen: Vandenhoeck & Ruprecht, 2d ed., 1966), pp. 52–53; for a good statement of the counterargument, see Bornkamm, "*presbyteros*," *TDNT*, Vol. 6, pp. 668–69.

8. This attempt is made by S. Läuchli, "Eine Gottesdienststruktur in der Johannesoffenbarung" *TZ* 16 (1960): 359–78; Massey Shepherd, *The Paschal Liturgy and the Apocalypse*, ESW 6 (1960).

specific formulas drawn from liturgical tradition.[9] But in each case the text is framed *ad hoc* for its particular context; it cannot be considered a predetermined component of common worship.[10] It is best not to speak at all of "hymns" in Revelation. Only in 5:9–10 and 15:3–4, the two passages where the author himself speaks of *ōdai*, is the acclamation associated with a motivation that is to a degree "hymnic" in nature; in their present form, however, not even these probably derive from public worship.[11] In other words, there is an inescapable aura of liturgical tradition in this prophetic book; but one can do justice to the situation only by distinguishing carefully between the structural elements employed and their concrete application and development.[12]

Much more dependent on developed liturgical tradition are the two deutero-Pauline epistles Colossians and Ephesians. This marks a significant difference from Paul, who frequently refers to kerygmatic and homological formulas, but only once, within the exhortation in Philippians 2, borrows a specifically liturgical text. In Colossians the hymn in 1:12–20, introduced by the word *eucharistountes*, "giving

9. Predications: Rev. 1:5, 8, 17*b*, 18; 2:8; 3:7, 14; and *passim;* doxologies: Rev. 1:5*b*, 6; 4:8*b*; 5:13*b*; and *passim;* acclamations: Rev. 4:11; 5:9, 12; 11:15; and *passim;* liturgical formulas: Rev. 4:8 (Trisagion) ; 5:14 (amen) ; 19:1, 3, 4, 6 (hallelujah) ; 22:20 (*Maranatha* in Greek translation) ; etc.

10. See G. Delling, "Zum gottesdienstlichen Stil der Johannes-Apokalypse," *NovT* 3 (1959) : 107–37.

11. At most one might still find in Rev. 5:9*b*, 10 a certain connection with liturgical discourse.

12. Even the frequent mention of a heavenly altar does not permit any inferences about the type of liturgical space used by the community.

thanks," lays the groundwork for the entire theological argument and the dispute with false doctrine.[13] It is furthermore noteworthy that the numerous baptismal passages exhibit a much more highly developed liturgical form.[14] Even the parenesis is noticeably liturgical in style, and in Colossians 3:16–17 we even find a specifically liturgical admonition.[15] It is also interesting that in the polemic against false doctrine[16] questions of proper worship arise far more often than in Galatians 4:9 ff. Among those who are teaching false doctrine, apart from their ob-

13. See E. Lohmeyer, *Die Briefe an die Kolosser und an Philemon*, KEK 9/2 (8th ed., 1930), pp. 40 ff., and the supplement by W. Schmauch in KEK 9 (13th ed., 1964), pp. 47 ff.; E. Käsemann, "A Primitive Christian Baptismal Liturgy," in his *Essays* (cited above, Chap. III, n. 8), pp. 149–68. For a history of scholarship on this passage, see H. J. Gabathuler, *Jesus Christus, Haupt der Kirche— Haupt der Welt*, ATANT 45 (1965); also N. Kehl, *Der Christushymnus im Kolosserbrief*, Stuttgarter biblische Monographien 1 (Stuttgart: Katholisches Bibelwerk, 1967); E. Lohse, *Colossians and Philemon*, trans. W. R. Poehlmann and R. J. Karris, Hermeneia (Philadelphia: Fortress, 1971), pp. 32 ff.; E. Schweizer, "Kolosser 1,15–20," in *Evangelisch-Katholischer Kommentar zum Neuen Testament; Vorarbeiten Heft 1* (Zurich: Benziger; Neukirchen-Vluyn: Neukirchener Verlag, 1969), pp. 7–31; R. Schnackenburg, "Die Aufnahme des Christushymnus durch den Verfasser des Kolosserbriefes," ibid., pp. 33–50; Sanders, *Christological Hymns* (cited above, Chap. VII, n. 14), pp. 9–12, 58–74; J. Reumann, "The 'Christ Hymn' of Colossians I," in *Christ and Humanity,* ed. Ivar Asheim (Philadelphia: Fortress, 1970), pp. 96–109; and Roy Harrisville, "The New Testament Witness to the Cosmic Christ," in *The Gospel and Human Destiny,* ed. Vilmos Vajta (Minneapolis: Augsburg, 1971), pp. 39–63.

14. The baptismal passages include the introduction to the hymn in Col. 1:12–14, as well as 1:21–22 (23) and the tradition in 2:20–3:4 which is expanded for polemic purposes.

15. This text cannot be discussed in detail here; see the commentaries and O. Söhngen, "Theologische Grundlagen der Kirchenmusik," in *Leiturgia* 4 (1961): 1–268, where the passage is discussed on pp. 3 ff.; idem, *Theologie der Musik* (Kassel: Johannes Stauda, 1967), pp. 12 ff.

16. Col. 2:4–3:4; for further discussion see G. Bornkamm, "Die Häresie des Kolosserbriefs," *TLZ* 78 (1948): cols. 11 ff., reprinted in his *Ende des Gesetzes* (cited above, Chap. VII, n. 44), pp. 139–56.

servance of festivals and days and regulations concerning purity and abstinence, the elements of *thrēskeia tōn angelōn* ("worship of angels") and *embateuein* (RSV, "taking his stand"; perhaps "enter into" a mystery cult) after the manner of the mysteries play a particularly important role.[17] In Ephesians there is no dispute with heretics, but dependence on liturgical and confessional tradition is even more striking than in Colossians, since entire sections are in large part only elaborations of existing material.[18] The first three chapters in particular are permeated with liturgical texts and baptismal traditions.[19] But even the parenetic passages in the three closing chapters exhibit, as in Colossians, marked dependence on liturgical formularies: Ephesians 5:14 is a summons

---

17. Col. 2:18, 23; see M. Dibelius and H. Greeven, *An die Kolosser, Epheser/An Philemon*, HNT 12 (3d ed., 1953), pp. 34 ff.

18. See G. Schille, *Liturgisches Gut im Epheserbrief* (Diss., Göttingen, 1953 [briefly summarized in Dibelius and Greeven, *An die Kolosser* (cited above, n. 17), pp. 112–13]); H. Schlier, *Der Brief an die Epheser* (Düsseldorf: Patmos, 1957), pp. 18–19, 123 n. 1; E. Käsemann, "Epheserbrief," in *RGG*, Vol. 2, cols. 517–20. On individual texts see E. Lohmeyer, "Das Proömium des Epheserbriefs," *ThBl* 5 (1926): 120–25; N. A. Dahl, "Adresse und Proömium des Epheserbriefs," *TZ* 7 (1951): 241–64; C. Maurer, "Der Hymnus in Eph 1 als Schlüssel zum ganzen Brief," *EvT* 11 (1951/52): 151–72; W. Nauck, "Eph 2, 19–22–ein Tauflied?" *EvT* 13 (1953): 362–71; J. Coutts, "Ephesians 1,3–14 and I Petr 1,3–12," *NTS* 3 (1956/57): 115–27; J. Cambier, "La Bénédiction d'Eph 1,3–14," *ZNW* 54 (1963): 58–104; J. Schattenmann, *Studien zum neutestamentlichen Prosahymnus* (Munich: Beck, 1965), pp. 1 ff.; Schille, *Hymnen* (cited above, Chap. VII, n. 14), pp. 65 ff.; and more recently F. Lang, "Die Eulogie in Epheser 1,3–14," in *Studien zur Geschichte und Theologie der Reformation* (Festschrift E. Bizer) (Neukirchen-Vluyn: Neukirchener, 1969), pp. 7–20.

19. The hymnic text Eph. 1:3–12 (13–14) is followed in the context of a *eucharistia* by confessional statements in 1:20–23, a baptismal tradition in 2:1–10, the markedly liturgical texts 2:14–18 and 2:19–22, and finally in 3:14–19, 20–21 a prayer with a doxology. See Jack T. Sanders, "Hymnic Elements in Ephesians 1–3," *ZNW* 56 (1965): 214–32; idem, *Christological Hymns* (cited above, Chap. VII, n. 14), pp. 14–15, 88–92.

taken from the baptismal liturgy,[20] and Ephesians 5:18–20 is a summons to proper worship in the Spirit borrowed from Colossians.[21] Ephesians 4:11 ff. also deserves notice: despite the already great emphasis on the special status of the apostles and prophets of the early period,[22] the structure of the community is maintained according to Paul's doctrine of charismata

When we turn to the Hellenistic Jewish Christianity of the subapostolic period which is independent of Paul, we must, in questions of community structure and worship, accord priority to Hebrews rather than to James and 1 Peter.[23] This appears above all in the structure of community leadership: according to Hebrews 13:7, it is in the hands of *hēgoumenoi, hoitines elalēsan hymin ton logon tou theou,* "leaders, who spoke to you the word of God."[24] As in the

20. In Ephesians 4–6 we find liturgically influenced texts primarily in the confessional statements in 4:4–6, the instructions concerning charismata in 4:11–16, the baptismal parenesis in 4:17–24; 5:8–14, as well as the section on spiritual panoply in 6:10–20. For a discussion of 5:14, see Schlier, *Epheser* (cited above, n. 18), pp. 240 ff.

21. Ephesians is dependent on Colossians, but in part transforms its model noticeably; see C. Leslie Mitton, *The Epistle to the Ephesians* (Oxford: Clarendon, 1951), pp. 55 ff.; Lohse, *Colossians* (cited above, n. 13), p. 4. Especially striking is the great emphasis on ecclesiology; cf. the reworking of Col. 1:24–27 in Eph. 3:1–13 and of Col. 3:18–4:1 in Eph. 5: (21) 22–6:9. See Franz Mussner, *Christus, das All und die Kirche,* Trierer Theologische Studien 5 (Trier: Paulinus, 1955), pp. 76 ff., 144 ff.

22. This status can be seen above all in Eph. 2:20 and 3:5 (cf. Col. 1:26).

23. This conclusion is independent of the dating of these documents; a later document can certainly represent an earlier stage of development. Like Revelation, 1 Peter must have been composed during the persecution of 95/96. It is more difficult to date Hebrews and James: they probably belong in the eighties or, at latest, the early nineties.

24. Cf. 13:17 and the description of the Epistle as *logos tēs paraklēseōs* ("word of exhortation") in 13:22. On the *hēgoumenoi,* see

deutero-Pauline writings just discussed, we find here that baptism has been accorded an augmented liturgical function; for the first time a confession of faith is clearly associated with baptism,[25] and the catechumenate, a decided innovation, is added.[26] A special problem is the neglect of assembly for worship and the emerging danger of apostasy, which is linked for the author of Hebrews with the impossibility of a second repentance and baptism.[27] When we come to the specifically "cultic" statements in 7:1–10:18,[28] we

Otto Michel, *Der Brief an die Hebräer,* KEK 13 (12th ed., 1966), pp. 488–89.

25. No text of the apostolic period associated baptism with a confession of faith. Only the cry "Abba" is connected with baptism (Rom. 8:15; Gal. 4:5–6). In Acts 8:37, the confession of faith is an addition from the western tradition. Only in Hebrews is the situation unambiguous: see Heb. 4:14; 10:23 ff.; also 6:4 ff.; and the discussion by G. Bornkamm, "Das Bekenntnis im Hebräerbrief," in his *Studien zu Antike und Urchristentum,* BEvT 28 (=his *Gesammelte Aufsätze* Band 2; 2d ed., 1963), pp. 188–203. On the hymn in 1:3, see Deichgräber, *Gotteshymnus* (cited above, Chap. VII, n. 14), pp. 137 ff.

26. See Heb. 5:11–6:3. Everywhere else, early Christian parenesis is postbaptismal in character, even in Heb. 10:19–13:19, as 10:22–23 clearly reveals. Of course *nēpioi* ("babes") are distinguished from *teleioi* ("the mature") even in 1 Cor. 3:1 ff.; but in Heb. 5:11 ff. this difference is clearly associated with the difference between the baptized and the unbaptized, and a prebaptismal catechumenate is associated with the *nēpioi*. Interestingly, the instruction of the "immature" comprises only themes deriving from or dealing with Jewish tradition (Heb. 6:1*b*, 2); there are no specifically Christian confessional statements, so that even here the *traditio symboli* (transmission of a creed) did not take place until baptism.

27. See Heb. 10:26–31, but also vv. 32 ff. and 6:4 ff. In the latter passage the problem dealt with is the impossibility of a second repentance and baptism, not "second penance" in the early ecclesiastical sense, however closely the two ideas are related; on this question, see Hans Windisch, *An die Hebräer,* HNT 14 (2d ed., 1930), pp. 52 ff.; Michel, *Hebräer* (cited above, n. 24), pp. 245 ff.

28. See M. Dibelius, "Der himmlische Kultus im Hebräerbrief," in his *Botschaft und Geschichte,* 2 vols. (Tübingen: Mohr, 1953–56), Vol. 2 (1956), pp. 160–76; U. Luck, "Himmlisches und irdisches Geschehen im Hebräerbrief," *NovT* 6 (1963): 192–215; W. Thüsing, "'Lasst uns hinzutreten . . .' (Hebr 10,22). Zur Frage nach dem Sinn der Kulttheologie im Hebräerbrief," *BZ* NF 9 (1965): 1–17.

find that the theme developed is the fulfillment and at the same time the abrogation of the Old Testament cult by Christ. This strikingly christological text should furthermore not be read apart from 12:18–29, where the ecclesiological conclusions are drawn from the one sacrifice of Christ: the faithful, as the community of the new covenant, are come to Mount Zion and the living city of God; they already belong to the "festal gathering" (12:22, *panēgyris*) with its words of praise and to the "assembly of the first-born."[29] Hebrews 13:15 therefore speaks of the "sacrifice of praise," and 13:9 ff. contrasts the *thysiastērion* (altar) to the table of the Lord's Supper.[30] The author is far from intending to give a special significance to the Lord's Supper or sacralize it, as the summons in 13:13 shows: *exerchōmetha pros auton exō tēs parembolēs,* "let us go forth to him outside the camp." Just as in the initial period and in Paul, the Lord's Supper and worship in general are looked upon as events that have their legitimate place outside the sacral and cultic sphere.[31] Despite the sporadic application of cultic terminology to the worship of the community, the Epistle to the Hebrews does anything but give occasion to speak of the claims of the cultic element" in Christian worship.[32]

The Epistle of James, apart from the statement in

29. See my exegesis of this text in *Göttinger Predigtmeditationen,* 20 (1965/66) : 74–84.

30. On the problems of this section see Michel, *Hebräer* (cited above, n. 24) , pp. 493 ff.

31. The author of Hebrews describes this sphere in 12:18–21!

32. *Pace* W. Hahn, *Gottesdienst* (cited above, Chap. I, n. 2) , pp. 136 ff. See below, pp. 105–8.

1:27 discussed above, contains a few references to church order and liturgical life only in its appendix (5:12–20). It presupposes the presbyterial form of government, which had already been adopted in the realm of Palestinian Jewish Christianity.[33] Besides the *psallein* ("to sing praise," 5:13) mentioned briefly in passing, it contains instructions on proper prayer, especially the "prayer of the righteous" that brings healing to a sick man, prayer which is reserved to the presbyters (5:14).[34]

Like Colossians and Ephesians, 1 Peter exhibits marked dependence on liturgical tradition and other fixed forms.[35] This is true of the *eulogia* ("blessing of God") in 1:3–12 and the baptismal traditions, as well as the associated christological and ecclesiological statements in 1:13–2:10.[36] Just as in Hebrews, the cultic terms in 2:5, 9–10 exhibit a contrast to tradi-

33. See Bornkamm, *"presbyteros," TDNT*, Vol. 6, p. 664.

34. For a detailed discussion, see M. Dibelius and H. Greeven, *Der Brief des Jakobus*, KEK 15 (11th ed., 1964), pp. 299 ff. The exhortation to pray rightly in faith (James 1:5–6) must be distinguished from these "liturgical" instructions. The relationship of the presbyters to the teachers mentioned in 3:1 remains unexplained. On the reference to baptism, see above, p. 63, especially n. 36.

35. See H. Windisch (and H. Preisker), *Die katholischen Briefe*, HNT 15 (3d ed., 1951), pp. 56–57, 65–66, 70 ff.; K. H. Schelkle, *Die Petrusbriefe/Der Judasbrief*, HTKNT 13/2 (1961), pp. 4 ff.; R. Bultmann, "Bekenntnis- und Liedfragmente im 1. Petrusbrief," in his *Exegetica* (Tübingen: Mohr, 1967), pp. 285–97. Under no circumstances is it possible to reconstruct an entire order of worship from 1 Peter, as was attempted by R. Perdelwitz, *Die Mysterienreligionen und das Problem des 1. Petrusbriefs*, Religionsgeschichtliche Versuche und Vorarbeiten 11/3 (Giessen: Töpelmann, 1911); H. Preisker, in his supplement to Windisch, op. cit., pp. 156 ff.; and F. L. Cross, *I Peter, A Paschal Liturgy* (London: Mowbray, 1954). Only isolated sections of the text derive from liturgical tradition.

36. An originally independent christological tradition is found in 1:18–19, 20, while the ecclesiological statements in 2:5–10 are firmly associated with the baptismal statements.

tional cultic and sacral notions, because we are here dealing once more with the status of the people of God within the world. It is not by accident, therefore, that the author includes parenetic traditions in 2:11–3:12 and 4:7–11.[37] There follows in 3:13–4:6 a section referring to the current situation of persecution, in which kerygmatic tradition has been incorporated; highly interesting is the interweaving of the reference to baptism with the confessional formulas in 3:18–22, a phenomenon that, like Hebrews 5:11 ff., suggests an explicit baptismal confession of faith.[38] In the concluding section (4:12 ff.), likewise structured independently by the author, the reference to presbyterial government is noteworthy; in 5:1 ff. 1 Peter thus shares common ground with James. But the charismatic gifts of the members of the community are not forgotten, as 4:10–11 shows; neither is there any trace of an incipient office superior to the presbyterate, since 5:1 even refers to Peter as a "fellow presbyter."[39]

The Pastoral Epistles exhibit a significantly more advanced stage of development. A late deutero-Pauline tradition has merged with the subapostolic tradition of Hellenistic Jewish Christianity just de-

37. The christological text 1 Pet. 2:21–25, heavily dependent on Isaiah 53, occupies a special position.

38. In 1 Pet. 3:18–22 (4:6), various types of formulaic material have been brought together; this section deserves more thorough analysis. In my opinion, it is impossible to follow Bultmann, "Bekenntnis - und Liedfragmente" (cited above, n. 35), in deriving a single prototype from the three christological texts in 1 Peter. On the problems of 3:18 ff., see Bo Reicke, *The Disobedient Spirits and Christian Baptism*, ASNU 13 (1946); W. J. Dalton, *Christ's Proclamation to the Spirits*, AnBib 23 (1965).

39. See Campenhausen, *Authority* (cited above, Chap. VII, n. 8), pp. 76 ff., especially 82–84; W. Nauck, "Probleme des frühchristlichen Amtsverständnisses (I Petr 5:2–3)," *ZNW* 48 (1957): 200–220.

scribed. Charismatic functions are consistently replaced by institutional office;[40] that rigid leadership of the community arose in the context of the bitter conflict with heretical groups does nothing to modify the gravity of this conclusion. It is clear that at first the presbyteries comprised the especially distinguished charismatics.[41] The gift of the Spirit long continued to be a requirement for appointment o office; but the view gradually prevailed that the laying on of hands[42] at the time of appointment conveyed a special charisma of office.[43] In addition, an

40. See the excursus in M. Dibelius and H. Conzelmann, *Die Pastoralbriefe*, HNT 13 (3d ed., 1955), pp. 44 ff.; also Campenhausen, *Authority* (cited above, Chap. VII, n. 8), pp. 76 ff., 106 ff.; Schweizer, *Church Order* (cited above, Chap. VII, n. 9), pp. 77 ff.; N. Brox, *Die Pastoralbriefe*, Regensburger Neues Testament 7/2 (Regensburg: Pustet, 4th ed., 1969), pp. 31 ff., 42 ff., 147 ff.

41. This point is correctly made by Campenhausen, *Authority* (cited above, Chap. VII, n. 8), p. 76.

42. The New Testament mentions the laying on of hands in three (four) contexts: healing, baptism, ordination, and (probably) the restoration of sinners (see the next note). Imposition of hands for healing has a separate significance and history. In baptism and ordination it is associated with the gift of the Spirit; the evidence for it in these contexts in primitive Christianity is relatively late: the redactional sections of Acts and the Pastoral Epistles (baptism: Acts 8:17; 9:17; 19:6; appointment to office: 1 Tim. 4:14; 2 Tim. 1:6; Acts 6:6; 13:3; most likely also Heb. 6:2). Jewish traditions have undoubtedly influenced ordination. See Johannes Behm, *Die Handauflegung im Urchristentum* (Leipzig: Deichert, 1911; 2d ed., Darmstadt: Wissenschaftliche Buchgesellschaft, 1968); N. Adler, *Taufe und Handauflegung*, NTA 19/3 (1951); E. Lohse, *Die Ordination im Spätjudentum und Urchristentum* (Göttingen: Vandenhoeck & Ruprecht, 1951); Brox, *Pastoralbriefe* (cited above, n. 40), pp. 181 ff. Dekkers suggests that the *prophēteia* mentioned in this context (1 Tim. 1:18; 4:14) is to be understood in the sense of *praefatio* or "a formula" (E. Dekkers, "PROPHĒTEIA—PRAEFATIO," in *Mélanges offerts à Christine Mohrmann* [1963], pp. 190–95; reference provided by my colleague Lengeling in Münster).

43. 1 Tim. 4:14; 2 Tim. 1:6. 1 Tim. 5:22*a* can hardly be included here, because vv. 20–21, 22*b* suggest that we are probably dealing with the restoration of sinners; see Bornkamm, "*presbyteros*," *TDNT*, Vol. 6, pp. 666–67. The introduction of a penitential institution during the subapostolic period can be recognized in Matt. 18:15–17; James 5:19–20; the summons to *elenchein* ("convince")

episkopos ("overseer," "bishop") now appears at the head of the presbytery as *primus inter pares*, although the relationship between *episkopos* and *presbyteroi* is not yet precisely fixed in the Pastoral Epistles.[44] This development had its effect on worship: henceforth this circle of official functionaries, especially the *episkopos,* is responsible for the conduct of worship.[45] Liturgical traditions are borrowed in the Pastorals alongside church orders and pareneses, as we see above all in the short hymn 1 Timothy 3:16,[46] the soteriological and baptismal text Titus 2:11–14; 3:4–7,[47] and the "ordination parenesis" 1 Timothy

in 2 Tim. 4:2; Titus 2:15 may likewise point to this institution (as in Matt. 18:15). Instructions to pray or not to pray for sinners (1 John 5:16 ff.) belong in the same context.

44. This can be seen above all when Titus 1:5–6 is compared with 1:7 ff. According to 1 Tim. 3:8 ff., *diakonoi* are associated with the *episkopos;* see Dibelius and Conzelmann, *Pastoralbriefe* (cited above, n. 40), pp. 44 ff.; Campenhausen, *Authority* (cited above, Chap. VII, n. 8), pp. 106 ff. The juxtaposition in Phil. 1:1 is to be understood differently; there, in imitation of Hellenistic prototypes, the *episkopoi* (plural!) have economic and financial functions, but no precedence or didactic function; see M. Dibelius, *An die Thessalonicher/An die Philipper* HNT 11 (3d ed., 1937), pp. 60–61. The beginnings of the monarchic episcopate found in the Pastorals are extremely complicated. The closest analogy is still the *m^rbaqqēr* of Qumran; see F. Nötscher, "Vorchristliche Typen urchristlicher Ämter? Episkopos und Mebaqqer," in his *Vom Alten und Neuen Testament (Gesammelte Aufsätze)* (Bonn: Hanstein, 1962), pp. 188–200; A. Adam, "Die Entstehung des Bischofsamtes" in *Jahrbuch der Theologischen Schule Bethel,* NF 5 (1957): 104–13; Herbert Braun, *Qumran und das Neue Testament,* 2 vols. (Tübingen: Mohr, 1966), Vol. 2, pp. 328 ff.

45. According to 1 Tim. 2:11–12, there is no place at all for women in the conduct of worship and in teaching. For the widows, however, 1 Tim. 5:3–16 creates a quasi-institutional position with certain diaconal functions; see Brox, *Pastoralbriefe* (cited above, n. 40), pp. 185 ff.

46. See Schweizer, *Lordship* (cited above, Chap. VII, n. 14), pp. 64 ff.; R. P. Martin, "Aspects of Worship in the New Testament Church," *Vox Evangelica* (essays by the faculty of London Bible College; London: Epworth Press) 2 (1963): 6–32.

47. See the excursus in Dibelius and Conzelmann, *Pastoralbriefe* (cited above, n. 40), pp. 108 ff.

6:11–16.[48] Also important is the mention in 1 Timothy 4:13 of *anagnōsis, paraklēsis,* and *didaskalia,* "public reading of scripture, preaching, and teaching." In this period, as we can demonstrate on the basis of other evidence to be discussed in a moment, scripture reading includes not only the Old Testament, but also specifically Christian documents.[49] *Paraklēsis* here refers to preaching in the general sense as exhortation, consolation, and admonition.[50] As the Pastoral Epistles show in other passages, *didaskalia* is critically important. The point is to preserve and transmit what has been entrusted (*parathēkē*; 1 Tim. 6:20; 2 Tim. 1:12,14), the "pure doctrine," inviolate, in the face of all heresies.[51] Thus the didactic element associated with episcopal office[52] received priority, as

48. E. Käsemann, "Das Formular einer neutestamentlichen Ordinationsparänese," in his *Exegetische Versuche* (cited above, Chap. VII, n. 14), Vol. i, pp. 101–8.

There is also the summons to prayer at 1 Tim. 2:1–3, where special mention is made of prayer for kings and all in authority (cf. 1 Clem. 60:4–61:2). This intercession on behalf of the authorities, which corresponds to Jewish tradition (cf. Jer. 29:7; Bar. 1:11–12; Pirqe Aboth 3:2), occupies the place in these parenetic sections that is occupied in Rom. 13:1–7 and 1 Pet. 2:17 by the summons to be subject to governmental authority. See Dibelius and Conzelmann, *Pastoralbriefe* (cited above, n. 40), pp. 30 ff.

49. See Paul Glaue, *Die Verlesung heiliger Schriften im Gottesdienst* (Berlin: Duncker, 1907) especially pp. 35 ff.; Nielen, *Liturgy* (cited above, Chap. I, n. 2), pp. 241–50, especially 247 ff. It is incorrect to assert that the reading of scripture came into being "to create a substitute for the messages presented by people endowed with the Spirit," as suggested by Leipoldt, *Gottesdienst* (cited above, Chap. I, n. 2), p. 48.

50. The term was already so used by Paul; see H. Schlier, "Vom Wesen der apostolischen Ermahnung," in his *Die Zeit der Kirche* (Freiburg: Herder, 1956), pp. 75 ff.; O. Schmitz, "*parakaleō, paraklēsis,*" in *TDNT*, Vol. 5, pp. 793–99.

51. 1 Tim. 1:10; 6:3; 2 Tim. 1:13; 4:3; Titus 1:9; 2:1; also 1 Tim. 6:20. See Dibelius and Conzelmann, *Pastoralbriefe* (cited above, n. 40), pp. 7 ff., 70; Brox, *Pastoralbriefe* (cited above, n. 40), pp. 107–8, 235–36.

52. According to 1 Tim. 3:2; Titus 1:9, the *episkopos* is expected to be a good teacher. The hypothesis of G. Holtz, *Die Pastoralbriefe*

even the style of these epistles shows. This priority involved significant structural changes and paved the way for the developments of the second century.[53]

Some interesting observations can be made concerning the reading of scripture in the subapostolic period. The composition of gospels[54] presupposes that reduction of oral traditions to written form was an obvious step, if not indispensable. Individual traditions and minor collections were frequently employed; for the most part they probably had their sitz im leben in preaching and instruction. The relatively extensive tradition of Jesus' passion, on the contrary, must have been reduced to written form even before Mark, for reading in the course of worship. Mark extends the passion narrative backward in time and takes the notion of the *euangelion* ("good news, gospel") as the dominant idea of his composition, likewise intended for liturgical use.[55] The extent to which liturgical use influenced the formation of Matthew's Gospel can be seen in many de-

THK 13 (1965), especially pp. 74–75, that the development of this office is associated with liturgical functions at the Lord's Supper, has no evidence to support it in the three Pastoral Epistles, but depends on texts that are much later.

53. The Pastoral Epistles must have been composed around the turn of the century at the latest; an unconvincing attempt has been made to date them later and identify the author with Polycarp of Smyrna (H. von Campenhausen, "Polycarp von Smyrna und die Pastoralbriefe" [Heidelberg: Winter, 1951], reprinted in his *Frühzeit* [cited above, Chap. VI, n. 16], pp. 197–252; idem, *Entstehung* [cited above, Chap. VI, n. 16], pp. 212–13).

54. The gospels were composed between A.D. 70 and 95: Mark around 70, Matthew in the eighties, Luke probably around 90, John between 90 and 95.

55. See Willi Marxsen, *Mark the Evangelist*, trans. J. Boyce et al (Nashville: Abingdon, 1969), pp. 117 ff.

tails.[56] Furthermore, borrowing Old Testament tradition, Matthew quite specifically terms his work a *biblos* ("book," 1:1). Luke likewise refers to a written work by his use of *diēgēsis* ("narrative"), but according to 1:4 he is thinking primarily in terms of catechetical use.[57] In this respect the conclusion of John is especially significant: in 20:30*b* we find the phrase *gegrammena en tō bibliō toutō* ("written in this book"), and in v. 31*a* the term *gegraptai* ("are written") otherwise reserved for Old Testament citations; this terminology points to the "scriptural" character of John's presentation without calling into question the richness and validity of the oral tradition that was still living.[58] In the deutero-Pauline doxology appended in Romans 16:25–27, there is a corresponding reference to the revelation of salvation and its disclosure "through prophetic scriptures," by which only early Christian documents can be meant. That the reading of the Pauline Epistles[59] soon led to

56. For further discussion see G. D. Kilpatrick, *The Origins of the Gospel according to St. Matthew* (Oxford: Clarendon, 1947), pp. 72 ff. In Matthew we can also see a clear difference between *kēryssein* in the sense of missionary proclamation and *didaskein* in the sense of preaching and instruction within the community; see especially Matt. 28:20. For a discussion, see Günther Bornkamm, "End-Expectation and Church in Matthew," in G. Bornkamm, G. Barth, and H. J. Held, *Tradition and Interpretation in Matthew*, trans. Percy Scott (Philadelphia: Westminster, 1963), p. 38, n. 1. Apart from the special meaning attached to *kēryssein*, it is interesting that *didaskein* still is understood in a sense that strongly emphasizes its sermonic character.

57. The significance of the critical key words in the Synoptics is clearly recognized by Marxsen, *Mark* (cited above, n. 55), pp. 25, 138 ff.; but he draws no conclusions with respect to the growth of scripture and its reading in primitive Christianity.

58. See the whole statement in John 20:30–31, especially v. 30*a*. John 21 is a deutero-Johannine supplement.

59. See C. Andresen, "Zum Briefformular frühchristlicher Gemeindebriefe," *ZNW* 56 (1965): 241 ff.

their being copied and collected is obvious. The
Revelation of John, too, with its canonization notice
in 22:18–19 expressly claims the status of sacred scripture.[60] This means that within the New Testament itself we can still trace the process of the growth of
scripture and see how an independent corpus of scripture began to develop. It also means in any case that
we may assume the liturgical reading of specifically
Christian scriptures in the subapostolic period.[61]

The Gospel of John and the Johannine Epistles
occupy a special position. They represent a position
in many respects independent of other developments
in the subapostolic period. It is true that we are dealing with a deliberately composed gospel document;
in the prologue of the Gospel a hymn is incorporated,[62] and the Epistles expressly oppose the fixed

60. See W. C. van Unnik, "De la règle *mēte prostheinai mēte
aphelein* dans l'histoire du canon," *VC* 3 (1949) : 1–36.
61. We encounter the reading of Christian scriptures as a regular
custom in Justin *Apology* 1. 67, which already bears witness to the
use of several gospel books. In the phrase *apomnēmoneumata tōn
apostolōn*, "memoirs of the apostles," the apologist Justin selected
a term that was not specifically Christian, instead equating the
gospels with memoir literature common in Hellenism; see K. L.
Schmidt, "Die Stellung der Evangelien in der allgemeinen Literatur-
geschichte," in *Eucharisterion* (Festschrift Gunkel), 2 vols., FRL-
ANT 36 (1923), Vol. 2, pp. 50–134. More illuminating for an understanding of the gospels within the Christian community is Irenaeus
Adv. haer. 3. 7–11, where the four-gospel canon is first mentioned;
see O. Cullmann, "The Plurality of the Gospels as a Theological
Problem in Antiquity," in his *The Early Church*, trans. S. Godman, ed. A. J. B. Higgins (Philadelphia: Westminster, 1956), pp.
39–58.
62. See E. Käsemann, "The Structure and Purpose of the Prologue
to John's Gospel," in his *Questions* (cited above, Chap. V, n. 17),
pp. 138–67; R. Schnackenburg, "Logos-Hymnus und johanneischer
Prolog," *BZ* NF 1 (1957) : 69–109; idem, *Johannesevangelium*
(cited above, Chap. III, n. 47), Vol. 1, pp. 197 ff.; E. Haenchen,
"Probleme des johanneischen 'Prologs'," in his *Gott* (cited above,

christological confession of faith to the teaching of heretics.[63] But there is no tendency to depend on any specifically liturgical tradition, nor is there any movement in the direction of an institutional organization of the community. These are points of contact between these documents and the Revelation of John, however fundamental may be the differences in the traditional material they incorporate and the fundamental theological attitudes they exhibit.[64] It is probably impossible to speak of any general use of liturgical symbolism in the Gospel of John.[65] Individual passages, however, present important fundamental statements about worship: for example, the conversation with Nicodemus about baptism (John 3:3 ff.),[66]

Chap. III, n. 47), pp. 114–43; C. Demke, "Der sogenannte Logos-Hymnus im johanneischen Prolog," *ZNW* 58 (1967) : 45–68; *pace* the assumption of a prototype by W. Eltester, "Der Logos und sein Prophet," in *Apophoreta* (cited above, Chap. V, n. 26), pp. 109–34. See also Brown, *John* (cited above, Chap. III, n. 47), Vol. 1, pp. 1–37, especially 21–23; Sanders, *Christological Hymns* (cited above, Chap. VII, n. 14), pp. 20–24, 29–57.

63. See 1 John 2:22–23; 4:2–3; 2 John 7.

64. Neither the Gospel of John nor the Epistles bear the stamp of any specifically Jewish Christian features; they are not even markedly dependent on apocalyptic tradition. If one wishes to speak of prophetic discourse in these documents, one must not overlook the fact that it differs markedly in form and content from the prophetic discourse of the Revelation of John. It is noteworthy in this regard that the term *prophēteuein* ("to prophesy") plays no role in the Gospel or the Epistles.

65. *Pace* Cullmann, *Worship* (cited above, Chap. I, n. 2), pp. 37 ff.; for the arguments against this view, see Wilhelm Michaelis, *Die Sakramente im Johannesevangelium* (Bern: BEG-Verlag, 1946). Further, Brown, *John* (cited above, Chap. III, n. 47), Vol. 1, pp. cxi–cxiv and *passim*.

66. Despite the text-critical uncertainty, the words *hydatos kai* ("water and") should probably not be eliminated from John 3:5, nor should the association with baptism be disputed. See Schnackenburg, *Johannesevangelium* (cited above, Chap. III, n. 47), Vol. 1, pp. 382–83; Brown, *John* (cited above, Chap. III, n. 47), Vol. 1, pp. 141–44.

the great bread discourse concerning the Lord's Supper (John 6:26 ff.),[67] and Jesus' conversation with the Samaritan woman about the proper way of worshiping God (John 4:19 ff.).[68] Of particular significance are the words concerning the Paraclete in the farewell discourses; apart from the statements about the relationship to the world, the crucial message is that the Holy Spirit is given to the faithful to bear witness, to lead them into all truth, and to remain with them.[69] By virtue of the operation of the Spirit the eschatological events continue, and God thus demonstrates his saving presence. Therefore we can even read in John 4:24 that "God is spirit." This is not meant to be understood in the sense of a definition of the concept of God, but as designating the reality and nearness of God in these revelatory events. Thus the proper worship of God can only be "in spirit and in truth." It is the Spirit that brings life and knowledge,[70] and the concept of "truth" is associated with

67. In John 6:51c–58, it is true, we have a later addition; see Bultmann, *John* (cited above, Chap. III, n. 33), pp. 234–37; and especially G. Bornkamm, "Die eucharistische Rede des Johannes-Evangeliums," *ZNW* 47 (1956) : 161–69, reprinted in his *Geschichte und Glaube I* (Gesammelte Aufsätze, vol. 3), BEvT 48 (1968), pp. 60–67. We cannot follow Bultmann in speaking of an "ecclesiastical redaction"; as in John 21, we are dealing with a deutero-Johannine addition. See also Brown, *John* (cited above, Chap. III, n. 47), Vol. 1, pp. 285–91.

68. In John 4 a narrative from Hellenistic Jewish Christian tradition has been utilized. The substance of the earlier tradition includes John 4:5–7, (8) 9 . . . 16–19, 20–26, 28–30, 40; vv. 20–26 have been revised by the evangelist. For a discussion of the analysis see Bultmann, *John* (cited above, Chap. III, n. 33), pp. 175–76, 179–80.

69. See John 14:16–17 (18–20), 26; 15:26–27; 16:7–11, 12–15. See G. Bornkamm, "Der Paraklet im Johannes-Evangelium," in his *Geschichte und Glaube I* (cited above, n. 67), pp. 68–89.

70. John 6:63; 14:17, 20.

the concrete revelatory event. Eschatological truth
has been revealed in Christ.[71] Therefore the Paraclete
is also called the "Spirit of truth," and it is said that
he will teach the community all things, but in doing
so remind them of Jesus' words.[72] In the Spirit and in
truth God's salvation is present.[73] Not only does this
spell the end of the Jerusalem temple and all other
cultic and sacral traditions, it also surmounts all religious antitheses. The age of true worship of God
has dawned.[74] The Johannine Epistles exhibit a more
conscious dependence on tradition,[75] but show at the
same time how the specifically Johannine fundamental understanding lives on. Despite the conflict with
false doctrine, charismatic organization of the community is not surrendered. As can be seen from 3
John, there was, to be sure, a serious conflict between
the author and Diotrephes, who represented organiza-

71. The term *alētheia* ("truth") is conceived christologically by
John: see above all 1:14,17 and 14:6, but also 5:33; 8:40 ff.; 18:37–38.
Pilate's response *ti estin alētheia;* ("What is truth?" 18:38) is not a
(skeptical) question about what truth is or can be, but a rejection of
the revealer.

72. See on the one hand John 14:17; 15:26; 16:13; on the other,
14:26.

73. John 4:19 ff. For a discussion of possible contacts with ideas
prevalent in the Qumran community see R. Schnackenburg,
"'Anbetung im Geist und in der Wahrheit' (Joh 4,23) im Lichte
der Qumran-Texte," *BZ* NF 3 (1959) : 88–94.

74. For a discussion of the individual problems of John 4, see
Bultmann, *John* (cited above, Chap. III, n. 33), pp. 176 ff.;
Schnackenburg, *Johannesevangelium* (cited above, Chap. III, n. 47),
Vol. 1, pp. 455 ff.; and Brown, *John* (cited above, Chap. III, n.
47), Vol. 1, pp. 164 ff., especially 175–76.

75. This is made especially clear by the use of the formula *ap'
archēs* ("from the beginning," 1 John 1:1); see H. Conzelmann,
"'Was von Anfang war'," in *Neutestamentliche Studien für Rudolf
Bultmann,* BZNW 21 (2d ed., 1957), pp. 194–201; not inaccurately
he terms 1 John a "Johannine pastoral epistle."

tion along official and institutional lines.[76] In the subsequent development of the early church, apart from Montanism, charismatic organization was soon forced completely into the background.[77]

The subapostolic period reveals an increasing use of developed liturgical traditions. The living charismatic structure of worship is in part already repressed by conscious adherence to liturgical formularies and an official organization of community leadership. At the same time scripture and instruction come to the fore. But the fundamental principle of primitive Christian worship is not yet surrendered: worship and service of God are based on the irruption of eschatological salvation. Crucial significance attaches to the surmounting of all limitation to a cultic and sacral sphere, and to the responsibility of the Christian within the world; these must now be maintained in the face of false doctrine.

76. See E. Käsemann, "Ketzer und Zeuge," *ZTK* 48 (1951): 168–87, reprinted in his *Exegetische Versuche* (cited above, Chap. VII, n. 14), Vol. 1, pp. 168–87; also the justified corrections by Bornkamm, *"presbyteros,"* *TDNT,* Vol. 6, p. 671, n. 121.

77. H. Kraft, "Die altkirchliche Prophetie und die Entstehung des Montanismus," *TZ* 11 (1955): 249–71. Here one can also include, despite certain distortions, the Christian prophets caricatured by Celsus; see Origen, *Contra Celsum* 7. 9; also the discussion in Leipoldt, *Gottesdienst* (cited above, Chap. I, n. 2), pp. 42–43. For their part, the Montanists could still appeal to a succession of prophets (Eusebius, *Hist. eccl.* 5. 17. 4). A part of the charismatic order was preserved later in the context of the concept of martyrdom; see K. Holl, "Die Vorstellung vom Märtyrer und die Märtyrerakten in ihrer geschichtlichen Entwicklung," in his *Aufsätze* (cited above, Chap. V, n. 36), Vol. 2 (1928), pp. 68–102.

IX

Worship in the
Apostolic Fathers and Justin

We can only touch on the Apostolic Fathers and Justin
Martyr in passing. They exhibit on the one hand the
continuing marked influence of the problems of the
subapostolic period, and on the other continued
rapid development and consolidation in the liturgical
area.[1]

The Didache[2] preserves the material that is tradition-historically earliest, although its content is far
from homogeneous. Here we find important information about liturgical life in the period ca. 80–130.[3]
In 4:1–2, for instance, we read about the liturgy of
the word, in chapter 7 about baptism, in chapter 8
about fasting and prayer, and in chapters 9–10 and
14 about the eucharist.[4] Chapter 14 also mentions the

1. See the brief but useful survey in Nagel, *Geschichte* (cited above,
Chap. I, n. 1), pp. 19 ff.
2. Rudolf Knopf, *Die Lehre der Zwölf Apostel,* HNT, Ergänzungs-
Band 1 (1920), pp. 1–40; J.-P. Audet, *La Didaché,* Études bibliques
(Paris: Gabalda, 1958).
3. This dating is independent of the question whether the document achieved its present form in the first or the second half of the
second century.
4. How many layers of tradition occur in the individual sections
can be illustrated from chapters 9–10 and 14. Three prayers constitute the basis of 9–10: the prayer over the cup, the prayer over
the broken bread, and also the thanksgiving for "spiritual food and
drink" (in certain cases including intercession for the church). In

"Day of the Lord," as well as introducing the still un-emphasized word *thysia* ("sacrifice") for the eucharist, which was soon to have momentous consequences.[5] Even more markedly than in the Pastoral Epistles we find the juxtaposition or superimposition of an earlier charismatic community organization (chapters 11–13) and an institutional form of leadership on its way to gaining the upper hand (chapter 15). It is interesting that in this case the transition took place without tension, because the charismatic talent fell into abeyance and the functions of the charismatics must have been taken over by the official leaders.[6]

In the Didache we already see instances in which the Jewish tradition of prayer has been borrowed.[7] In the subsequent period we encounter this borrowing more frequently and much more extensively. A

my opinion, these correspond best to the primitive Christian observance of Passover; see my "Motive" (cited above, Chap. III, n. 17), pp. 352 ff., especially p. 357, n. 69. Did. 10:6b is an ancient formula of admission; its attachment to the prayers reveals that the action of the bread and cup was transferred to the end of the meal (with Mark 14:22–25/Matt. 26:26–29, in contrast to the Pauline and Lukan tradition which has the phrase *meta to deipnēsai*, "*after* supper*" at 1 Cor. 11:25 and Luke 22:20, separating the action with the bread from the action with the cup). The significantly later formula of admission in 9:5 and its present position, as well as the superscription in 9:1, show clearly that the association with Passover was no longer understood; here we are probably already dealing with a "eucharist" separate from the festival meal. For a different interpretation, see A. Adam, "Erwägungen zur Herkunft der Didache," *Zeitschrift für Kirchengeschichte* 68 (1957): 1–47, especially pp. 9 ff., and Goppelt, *Apostolic . . . Times* (cited above, Chap. I, n. 5), pp 46 f., 212–13; they both think in terms of prayers at an agape celebration.

5. Did. 13:3 also refers, without particular emphasis, to the prophets as high priests.

6. See Campenhausen, *Authority* (cited above, Chap. VII, n. 8), pp. 72 ff.; Schweizer, *Church Order* (cited above, Chap. VII, n. 9), pp. 139–45.

7. See M. Dibelius, "Die Mahlgebete der Didache," *ZNW* 37 (1938): 32–41, reprinted in his *Botschaft* (cited above, Chap. VIII, n. 28), Vol. 2 (1956), pp. 117–27.

first important example is the great intercessory prayer in 1 Clement.[8] In the New Testament we can find dependence on forms and individual elements, but never any borrowing of the text of entire prayers. Now by the end of the first century, as 1 Clement, composed in the nineties, shows, Jewish prayers were certainly being borrowed; during the second and third centuries the church made increasing use of Jewish liturgical tradition to develop its liturgy, as can be seen above all in the early church orders and services.[9] In 1 Clement we also encounter the Trisagion in its original Old Testament form, which was still current in Judaism;[10] in Revelation 4:8 it had appeared in a Christianized form which was typical

---

8. 1 Clem. 59:2*b*–61:3; for discussion, see R. Knopf, *Die zwei Clemensbriefe*, HNT, Ergänzungs-Band 1 (1920), pp. 137 ff.; also E. von der Goltz, *Das Gebet in der ältesten Christenheit* (Leipzig: Hinrichs, 1901), pp. 196 ff.; Otto Knoch, *Eigenart und Bedeutung der Eschatologie im theologischen Aufriss des ersten Clemensbriefes*, Theophaneia 17 (Bonn: Hanstein, 1964), pp. 61 ff.

9. See P. Drews, *Studien zur Geschichte des Gottesdienstes II/III: Untersuchungen über die sogenannte klementinische Liturgie im VIII. Buch der Apostolischen Konstitutionen* (Tübingen: Mohr, 1960); W. Bousset, "Eine jüdische Gebetssammlung im siebenten Buch der Apostolischen Konstitutionen," in *Nachrichten von der Gesellschaft der Wissenschaften zu Göttingen* (1915), pp. 435–89; Lietzmann, *Entstehung* (cited above, Chap. I, n. 1), pp. 3–27, especially pp. 4 ff.

10. Cf. Isa. 6:3; Enoch (Eth.) 39:2; and the so-called *quedusha* (here associated with Ezek. 3:12); besides 1 Clem. 34:4, see also *Apostolic Constitutions* 8. 12. 27*b*. For discussion, see W. C. van Unnik, "1 Clement 34 and the 'Sanctus'," *VC* 5 (1951): 204–48; G. Kretschmar, *Studien zur frühchristlichen Trinitätslehre*, Beiträge zur historischen Theologie, 21 (Tübingen: Mohr, 1956), pp. 134 ff.; D. Flusser, "Sanctus und Gloria," in *Abraham unser Vater* (Festschrift Michel), AGSU 5 (1963), pp. 128–63; P. Prigent, *Apocalypse et Liturgie*, Cahiers théologique 52 (Neuchatel: Delachaux et Niestlé, 1964), pp. 56 ff.; A. Adam, *Lehrbuch der Dogmengeschichte*, 2 vols. (Gütersloh: Mohn, 1965–68), Vol. 1 (1965), pp. 117 ff.; also J. A. Jungmann, *Mass* (cited above, Chap. I, n. 8), Vol. 2, p. 132, n. 26 (2d ed. abridged, p. 381, with the note omitted).

of the author of that document. In addition to these
borrowings from Jewish tradition, 1 Clement also
contains characteristic innovations. As in the Didache,
for example, certain expressions deriving from the
sacrificial cult are applied to the eucharist.[11] Furthermore, the necessity for an avowedly cultic order is
now demonstrated with the aid of scriptural proofs
based on the Old Testament.[12]

The situation becomes even more difficult in Ignatius of Antioch. On the one hand, he represents a
strictly monarchic episcopate, allowing only the
bishop to officiate at celebration of the eucharist;[13] on
the other, he accepts a massive sacramentalism, as
appears above all in his view of the Lord's Supper.[14]

In none of these extant texts can we demonstrate
the existence of a common basic form for Christian
worship. It is also questionable whether before the
middle of the second century there was already any
fixed liturgical order and a "unified form of worship." The letter of Pliny the Younger, which dates
between 111 and 113, can hardly presuppose a baptismal liturgy in the early morning and a unified
basic liturgy in the evening; in the morning the community assembles for prayer, praise, and proclamation of the word, while it celebrates the Lord's Sup-

11. 1 Clem. 36:1; 44:4.

12. 1 Clem. 40:2–5; see J. A. Fischer, *Die Apostolischen Väter*
(Munich: Kösel, 1956), p. 15; Nagel, *Geschichte* (cited above,
Chap. I, n. 1), pp. 20–21.

13. Smyrn. 8; cf. Phld. 4.

14. Eph. 20:2; Smyrn. 7:1. For a discussion of Ignatius, see W. Bauer,
Die Briefe des Ignatius von Antiochien, HNT, Ergänzungs-Band 2
(1920); H. W. Bartsch, "Ignatius von Antiochien," in *RGG*, Vol.
3, cols. 665–67 (with bibliography). The Epistles of Ignatius incorporate much formulaic material that deserves thorough study.

per in the evening.[15] Evening assembly to celebrate the Lord's Supper in connection with a regular meal is the usual form in the New Testament. Not until Justin is the ritual of the bread and cup separated from the meal as the "eucharist" and incorporated into Sunday morning worship. Here the unified form of worship achieves its fundamental and henceforth binding form.[16] The separation of the eucharist from the fellowship meal corresponds on the other hand to the development of the so-called agape, which is most likely mentioned in one of the latest documents of the New Testament, the Epistle of Jude.[17] We may assume that Justin was not the first to give early Christian worship its definitive form, and that this form came to prevail some time before his *Apology* was written.[18] But the beginnings of this form can be traced back no earlier than the twenties of the second century, and it was probably not firmly established until the middle of the century.

15. See H. Lietzmann, "Die liturgischen Angaben des Plinius," in his *Kleine Schriften*, ed. Kurt Aland, 3 vols., TU 67, 68, 74 (1958–62), Vol. 3 (1962), pp. 48–53; R. P. Martin, "A Footnote to Pliny's Account of Christian Worship," *Vox Evangelica* (cited above, Chap. VIII, n. 46) 3 (1964): 51–57; idem, "The Bithynian Christians' Carmen Christo," *Studia patristica* 3, TU 93 (1966). pp. 259–68; Paul Winter, "Tacitus and Pliny: The Early Christians," *Journal of Historical Studies* 1 (1967): 31–40.

16. See R. Stählin, "Die Geschichte des christlichen Gottesdienstes," *Leiturgia* 1 (1954): 1–82, especially pp. 17 ff.; Nagel, *Geschichte* (cited above, Chap. I, n. 1), pp. 27 ff.

17. Jude 12. The Epistle of Jude was probably composed between 120 and 140, 2 Peter, which depends on it, around the middle of the century. The earliest formulary for the celebration of an agape occurs in the church order of Hippolytus, chapter 47; see B. Botte, *La tradition apostolique de Saint Hippolyte*, Liturgiewissenschaftliche Quellen und Forschungen 39 (Münster: Aschendorff, 1962).

18. The *Apology* was composed around A.D. 165.

X

Conclusions

When we look back over the history of early Christian worship, which can be recognized in outline, the wealth of individual traditions and their often very diverse developments force us to raise the question of where their unity lies; but this same diversity precludes any facile answer. The New Testament traditions cannot be summarized on a single plane; neither can the form of unified worship that crystallizes during the second century be considered the only possible and necessary outcome. Here we find the beginning of the history that has put its stamp on the worship of the Christian church over the course of centuries; but the price paid was the loss of the original wealth and of liturgical vitality. We cannot simply reach back to the worship of the primitive church. The New Testament evidence cannot be made normative in the sense that the various elements and forms must all be recovered and imitated. They must, however, provide a model for renovation and restructuring in the face of all adherence to a later, historically developed form of worship, in the face of all traditionalism and legalism in liturgical matters. The proper form of worship is always proper only to its own age, because only thus can the missionary function of worship and its function in equipping the faithful for service in the world be taken seriously. In this process the crucial principles of the New Testament understanding of worship must be vindicated anew theologically and given appropriate expression. The following points are essential.

(1) The Christian community assembles for worship on the basis of God's eschatological saving act in Christ, which demonstrates its present power in the operation of the Spirit. It is proper to speak of "salvific action in worship"[1] to the extent that the various forms of proclamation of the word, the performance of baptism, and the celebration of the Lord's Supper are all concerned with the "service of God to the community," to which corresponds the "service of the community before God" in obedience, prayer, and confession of faith.[2] But the fact must not be ignored that proclamation of the word, baptism, and Lord's Supper are brought to men, and thus take the form of human service.

(2) In worship the *oikodomē* ("edifying, upbuilding") of the church takes place. Within the community of the faithful the new creation takes concrete, bodily form for the salvation of the world. Therefore worship has by nature a missionary function. It is and remains open to all who do not believe.[3]

1. Peter Brunner, "Zur Lehre vom Gottesdienst der im Namen Jesu versammelten Gemeinde," *Leiturgia* 1 (1954): 83–361, especially pp. 181 ff.; *Worship in the Name of Jesus,* trans. M. H. Bertram (St. Louis: Concordia, 1968), especially pp. 109 ff.
2. Ibid., pp. 253 ff. A similar idea is expressed by Lohmeyer, *Lord of the Temple* (cited above, Chap. I, n. 7), p. 6: "All cultic activity on the part of man is merely *re-actio* to God's *actio,* the response *(Antwort)* to His preceding word *(Wort)*." See also W. Hahn, *Gottesdienst* (cited above, Chap. I, n. 2), pp. 40 ff., 134, and *passim.*
3. W. Nagel once stated orally: "Worship must take its shape from the *apistos* [the unbeliever]."

(3) For the Christian community worship does not take place in a separate realm but in the midst of the existing world; it therefore includes service by the faithful in everyday life. Christian worship is no longer cultic in nature. "Just as Jesus Christ is the end of the law He is also the end of the cult."[4] It does not help to come up with as broad a generalization as possible of the term "cult,"[5] or to assume the "establishment of a new cult";[6] such expedients do not adequately express the fundamental difference between Christian worship and the cults of pagan antiquity, or even the cult of Old Testament Judaism with its sacred precincts, its ritual regulations, and its sacrificial system.[7] The transferred use of cultic terminology in the New Testament is always con-

4. Edmund Schlink, "Worship from the Viewpoint of Evangelical Theology," in *The Coming Christ and the Coming Church*, trans. I. H. Neilson et al. (Philadelphia: Fortress, 1968), p. 133. The passage continues: "That Christ is the end of the law does not of course mean that He was the end of divine rule. But God's commandment encounters believers in the Gospel no longer as the law but as the Paraclete [German, *Paraklese*, 'encouragement'], as comforting, fatherly exhortation. . . . That Christ is the end of the cult means just as little that He was the end of divine worship. Something so completely new takes place now in him that the old names no longer suffice" (pp. 133–34).

5. S. Mowinckel, *Religion und Kultus* (Göttingen: Vandenhoeck & Ruprecht, 1953), pp. 10 ff.; idem, "Kultus," in *RGG*, Vol. 4, cols. 120–26.

6. Lohmeyer, *Lord of the Temple* (cited above, Chap. I, n. 7), p. 5: we are dealing with a cult that "embraces the whole of revelation and of faith"; pp. 104–5: the eschatological overcoming of the old and the establishment of the new cult is expressed most profoundly in the institution of the Lord's Supper, which is associated with the establishment of the new community. Therefore "the question of the foundation of a new cult cannot be answered in a simple yes *or* no but only in a profound, eschatologically determined yes *and* no."

7. These three elements (sacred place, ritual, and sacrifice) are determinative for the concept of "cult"; but even if one were to separate out the sacrificial component, the concept would not be appropriate or acceptable for Christian worship.

sciously polemic in nature.[8] This holds true especially of the idea of sacrifice: when Old Testament sacrificial terminology is applied to the Christ-event[9] or even to human actions,[10] we are dealing with the abolition of the traditional sacrificial cult by the eschatological operation of God.[11]

(4) Worship can be properly ordered only when the freedom necessary for the operation of the Spirit remains. All legalism is contrary to the nature of the worship performed by the community assembled in the name of Jesus. But this means at the same time that worship must as much as possible be kept free of rigid institutional order. It is true that Spirit and law, charisma and order, are not mutually exclusive;[12] but when office and community organization are fixed by formal law, we have probably reached that fateful limit of institutionalization that usually leaves no room for the manifold gifts of the Spirit.[13]

8. That Christian worship must repeatedly overcome the ever-present tendency to become cultic by virtue of the contemporization of the eschatological event has been strikingly demonstrated by Götz Harbsmeier, "Das Problem des Kultischen im evangelischen Gottesdienst," in his *Dass wir die Predigt und sein Wort nicht verachten* (Gesammelte Aufsätze) (Munich: Kaiser, 1958), pp. 11–40.

9. See above, p. 62, n. 29.

10. In parenesis, for example, and in the liturgical passages 1 Pet. 2:5; Heb. 13:15.

11. *Pace* Hahn, *Gottesdienst* (cited above, Chap. I, n. 2), p. 24 and *passim*, we must maintain that in the sense just described the New Testament is absolutely "anticultic." The isolated use of cultic categories to speak of the Christ-event does not permit us in principle to speak of the revelation of Christ as a "cultic event" (p. 132), the more so because this view, deriving from the Epistle to the Hebrews, leaves the important passage 12:18–25a out of consideration (in 12:22–25a there are, characteristically, no cultic terms).

12. See above, p. 72, n. 25.

13. The relationship between "institution and event" cannot be balanced as simply as J. L. Leuba attempts to do in his 1950 book by the same title, *L'institution et l'événement* (Neuchatel: Delachaux et Niestlé 1950; Eng. trans. Harold Knight, *New Testament*

(5) The worship of Christians is dominated by God's eschatological gift of salvation, and remains open to God's future acts. It concerns both the future that God ever gives anew to his community in this world and the expectation of the consummation. Thus Christian worship is the responsible service of those that have put their hand to the plow and do not look back, but with burning hearts join in the cry, "Maranatha, our Lord, come."

Pattern [London: Lutterworth, 1953]); see the pointed criticism by E. Käsemann in *Verkündigung und Forschung 1956/57* (1959) : 163–67. B. C. Butler, "Spirit and Institution in the New Testament," *Studia Evangelica*, 3/2, TU 88 (1964) , pp. 138–65, even sees ecclesiastical institutions as given in the very earliest beginnings of the church and attempts to trace them back to Jesus, thus also evading the actual problem. However much in error Sohm's total presentation in *Kirchenrecht I* may be, we cannot evade the question he raises so clearly of how we are to judge the transition from the structure of the primitive Christian community to the governmental system of the early Catholic church.

For Further Reading

I. BIBLIOGRAPHY OF WORKS BY PROFESSOR HAHN:

Christologische Hoheitstitel. Ihre Geschichte im frühen Christentum. FRLANT 83. Göttingen: Vandenhoeck & Ruprecht, 1963; 3d ed., 1966. English: *The Titles of Jesus in Christology: Their History in Early Christianity.* Trans. Harold Knight and George Ogg. London: Lutterworth, and New York and Cleveland: World Publishing Company, 1969.

Major analyses of *Christologische Hoheitstitel:*

VIELHAUER, PHILIPP. "Zur Frage der christologischen Hoheitstitel." *TLZ* 90 (1965): col. 569–88. *NT Abstracts* 10, No. 762r.

———. "Jesus und der Menschensohn. Zur Diskussion mit Heinz Eduard Tödt und Eduard Schweizer." *ZNW* 60 (1963) : 133–77. *NTAbstracts* 8, No. 920. Reprinted in his *Aufsätze zum Neuen Testament.* ThBü 31. Munich: Kaiser, 1965. Pp. 92–140.

———. "Ein Weg zur neutestamentlichen Christologie? Prüfung der Thesen Ferdinand Hahns." *EvT* 25 (1965) : 24–72. *NTAbstracts* 9, No. 1145r. Reprinted with minor revisions in his *Aufsätze* (cited above). Pp. 141–98.

KOESTER, W. "Zur Geschichte der christologischen Hoheitstitel." *Scholastik* (Freiburg) 40 (1965) : 91–103. *NTAbstracts* 9, No. 1144r.

Das Verständnis der Mission im Neuen Testament. WMANT 13. Neukirchen-Vluyn: Neukirchener Verlag, 1963; 2d ed., 1965. (New ed. in preparation.) English:

Mission in the New Testament. Trans. Frank Clarke. SBT 47. London: SCM, and Naperville: Allenson, 1965.

(With Günther Bornkamm and Wenzel Lohff) *Die Frage nach dem historischen Jesus.* Evangelisches Forum 2. Göttingen: Vandenhoeck & Ruprecht, 1962, ²1966. Pp. 7–40. English: *What Can We Know about Jesus? Essays on the New Quest.* Trans. Grover Foley. Philadelphia: Fortress, 1969 (paper). Pp. 9–48, "The Quest of the Historical Jesus and the Special Character of the Sources Available to Us."

(With August Strobel and Eduard Schweizer) *Die Anfänge der Kirche im Neuen Testament.* Evangelisches Forum 8, ed. Paul Rieger. Göttingen: Vandenhoeck & Ruprecht, 1967. English: *The Beginnings of the Church in the New Testament.* Trans. Iain and Ute Nicol. Edinburgh: Saint Andrew Press, and Minneapolis: Augsburg, 1970 (paper). Pp. 9–39, "Pre-Easter Discipleship."

"Die alttestamentlichen Motive in der urchristlichen Abendmahlsüberlieferung." *EvT* 27 (1967): 337–74. *NTAbstracts* 12, No. 694.

(With Gerhard Sauter) *Verantwortung für das Evangelium in der Welt: EKD-Synodalreferat 1970 und Kommentar.* Theologische Existenz heute, NF 167. Munich: Kaiser, 1970. Pp. 9–37, "Die Verantwortung für das Evangelium in die Welt" (with theses).

"Das Gleichnis von der Einladung zum Festmahl." In *Verborum Veritas* (Festschrift Gustav Stählin). Wuppertal: R. Brockhaus, 1970. Pp. 51–82.

"Das Problem 'Schrift und Tradition' im Urchristentum." *EvT* 30 (1970): 449–68. *NTAbstracts* 15, No. 405.

"Der Prozess Jesu nach dem Johannesevangelium." *Evangelisch-Katholischer Kommentar zum Neuen Testament, Vorarbeiten Heft 2.* Zurich: Benziger, and Neukirchen-Vluyn: Neukirchener Verlag, 1970. Pp. 23–96.

"Methodenprobleme einer Christologie des Neuen Testaments." *Verkündigung und Forschung* 15 (1970) : 3–41.

"Die Sendschreiben der Johannesapokalypse. Ein Beitrag zur Bestimmung prophetischer Redeformen." In *Tradition und Glaube. Das frühe Christentum in seiner Umwelt. Festgabe für Karl Georg Kuhn zum 65. Geburtstag.* Ed. G. Jeremias, H. W. Kuhn, and Hartmut Stegemann. Göttingen: Vandenhoeck & Ruprecht, 1971. Pp. 357–94.

"Die Bildworte vom neuen Flicken und vom jungen Wein (Mk. 2, 21f parr)." *EvT* 31 (1971) : 357–75. *NT-Abstracts* 16, No. 548.

"Genesis 15,6 im Neuen Testament." In *Probleme biblischer Theologie: Gerhard von Rad zum 70. Geburtstag.* Ed H. W. Wolff. Munich: Chr. Kaiser, 1971. Pp. 90–107.

"Sehen und Glauben im Johannesevangelium." In *Neues Testament und Geschichte: Historisches Geschehen und Deutung im Neuen Testament* (Festschrift Oscar Cullmann). Ed. Heinrich Baltensweiler and Bo Reicke. Zurich: Theologischer Verlag, and Tübingen: Mohr, 1972. Pp. 124–41.

"Probleme historischer Kritik." *ZNW* 63 (1972) : 1–17.

II. BIBLIOGRAPHY CHOSEN BY PROFESSOR HAHN ON THE SUBJECT OF THIS BOOK:

A. New Testament

WEIZSÄCKER, KARL HEINRICH VON. *Das Apostolische Zeitalter der christlichen Kirche.* Tübingen: Mohr, 1889; 3d ed., 1902. Pp. 546–83. English: *The Apostolic Age of the Christian Church.* 2 vols. Trans. James Millar. Theological Translation Library, 1, 5. London: Williams & Norgate; New York: Scribner, 1894–1895. Especially Vol. 2: Theological Translation Library 5 (1895), pp. 246–90.

BAUER, WALTER. *Der Wortgottesdicnst der ältesten Christen.* Sammlung gemeinverständlicher Vorträge und Schriften aus dem Gebiet der Theologie und Religionsgeschichte, 148. Tübingen: Mohr, 1930. Reprinted in his *Aufsätze und kleine Schriften.* Ed. Georg Strecker. Tübingen: Mohr, 1967. Pp. 155–209.

MACDONALD, ALEXANDER BUCHANAN. *Christian Worship in the Primitive Church.* Edinburgh: Clark, 1934.

LEIPOLDT, JOHANNES. *Der Gottesdienst der ältesten Kirche.* Leipzig: Dörffling & Franke, 1937.

NIELEN, JOSEF MARIA. *Gebet und Gottesdienst im Neuen Testament.* Freiburg: Herder, 1937; 2d ed., 1963. English: *The Earliest Christian Liturgy.* Trans. P. Cummins. St. Louis: Herder, 1941 .

LOHMEYER, ERNST. *Kultus und Evangelium.* Göttingen: Vandenhoeck & Ruprecht, 1942. English: *Lord of the Temple.* Trans. S. Todd. Edinburgh: Oliver & Boyd, 1961.

CULLMANN, OSCAR. *Urchristentum und Gottesdienst.* ATANT 3. 2d ed., Zurich: Zwingli, 1950; 4th ed., 1962. English: *Early Christian Worship.* Trans. A. S. Todd and J. B. Torrance. SBT 10. Chicago: Regnery; London: SCM, 1953; 2d ed., 1962.

KOOLE, JAN LEUNIS. *Liturgie en Ambt in de apostolische Kerk.* Kampen: J. K. Kok, 1949.

HAHN, WILHELM TRAUGOTT. *Gottesdienst und Opfer Christi.* Berlin: Evangelische Verlagsanstalt, 1951.

DELLING, GERHARD. *Der Gottesdienst im Neuen Testament.* Göttingen: Vandenhoeck & Ruprecht, 1952. English: *Worship in the New Testament.* Trans. Percy Scott. Philadelphia: Westminster; London: Darton, Longmans, 1962.

MÜLLER-BARDORFF, J. *Wesen und Werden des christlichen Gottesdienstes im apostolischen Zeitalter.* Habilitationsschrift, Leipzig, 1953.

CRANFIELD, C. E. B. "Divine and Human Action: The Biblical Concept of Worship." *Interpretation* 22 (1958) : 387–98.

REICKE, BO IVAR. "Some Reflections on Worship in the New Testament," in *New Testament Essays (Studies in Memory of Thomas Walter Manson).* Manchester: Manchester University Press, 1959. Pp. 194–209.

HAMMAN, A. *La prière. I. Le Nouveau Testament.* Bibliothèque de théologie. Tournai: Desclée, 1959. English: *Prayer—First Three Centuries of the Christian Church.* Trans. P. J. Oligny. Chicago: Franciscan Herald Press, 1971.

MOULE, CHARLES FRANCIS DIGBY. *Worship in the New Testament.* ESW 9. London: Lutterworth; Richmond: John Knox, 1961.

RORDORF, WILLY. *Der Sonntag.* ATANT 43. Zurich: Zwingli, 1962. English: *Sunday: The History of the Day of Rest and Worship in the Earliest Centuries of the Christian Church.* Trans. A. A. K. Graham. Philadelphia: Westminster, 1968.

MARTIN, RALPH P. *Worship in the Early Church.* London: Marshall, Morgan & Scott, 1964.

KRAUS, HANS JOACHIM. "Gottesdienst im alten und neuen Bund." *EvT* 24 (1964): 171-206.

LEHMANN, O. "Communal Worship in the New Testament and Contemporary Rabbinical Literature." Second International Congress on New Testament Studies, Oxford, 1961. *Studia Evangelica 3.* TU 88. Berlin: Akademie Verlag, 1964. Pp. 246–49.

SCHWEIZER, EDUARD. "Gottesdienst im Neuen Testament und Kirchenbau heute." *Die Zeichen der Zeit* 11 (1965) : 393-400. Reprinted in *Beiträge zur Theologie des Neuen Testaments (Neutestamentliche Aufsätze 1955–1970).* Zurich: Zwingli, 1970. Pp. 249–62.

———. "Gottesdienst im Neuen Testament und heute (Gerhard Delling zum 65. Geburtstag am 10. Mai

1970) ." First published in his *Beiträge* (cited in previous entry), pp. 263–82.

CONZELMANN, HANS. "Christus im Gottesdienst der neutestamentlichen Zeit." *Monatsschrift für Pastoraltheologie* 55 (1966): 355–65.

STENDAHL, KRISTER. *The Bible and the Role of Women: A Case Study in Hermeneutics*. FBBS 15. Trans. Emilie T. Sander. Philadelphia: Fortress, 1966. Bibliography on women in the New Testament.

SCHWEIZER, EDUARD. "Abendmahl, I. Im NT." *RGG*, Vol. 1, cols. 10–21. English: *The Lord's Supper According to the New Testament*. FBBS 18. Trans. James M. Davis. Philadelphia: Fortress, 1967. Extensive bibliography on the eucharist.

MARXSEN, WILLI. *Das Abendmahl als christologisches Problem*. Gütersloh: Gütersloher Verlagshaus Gerd Mohn, 1963. English: *The Lord's Supper as a Christological Problem*. FBBS 25. Trans. Lorenz Nieting. Philadelphia: Fortress, 1970. Additional bibliography. Treats development of the eucharist on a tradition-history basis.

B. *The Liturgy of the Early Church*

HARNACK, THEODOR. *Der christliche Gemeindegottesdienst im apostolischen und altkatholischen Zeitalter*. Erlangen: Bläsing, 1854.

PROBST, FERDINAND. *Liturgie der drei ersten christlichen Jahrhunderte*. Tübingen: Laupp, 1870. Reprinted, Darmstadt: Wissenschaftliche Buchgesellschaft, 1968.

KÖSTLIN, H. A. *Geschichte des christlichen Gottesdienstes*. Freiburg: Mohr, 1887.

DUCHESNE, LOUIS MARIE OLIVIER. *Origines du culte chrétien*. Paris: Fontemoing, 1889; 5th ed., 1925. English: *Christian Worship: Its Origin and Evolution*. Trans. M. L. McClure. London: SPCK, 1903.

RENDTORFF, FRANZ. *Geschichte des christlichen Gottes-dienstes unter dem Gesichtspunkt der liturgischen Erbfolge. Ein Grundlegung der Liturgik.* Studien zur praktischen Theologie, 7. Giessen: Töpelmann, 1914.

WETTER, GILLIS PETERSSON. *Altchristliche Liturgien.* 2 vols. FRLANT 13, 17. Göttingen: Vandenhoeck & Ruprecht, 1921–1922.

BAUMSTARK, ANTON. *Vom geschichtlichen Werden der Liturgie.* Ecclesia orans, 10. Freiburg: Herder, 1923.

LIETZMANN, HANS. *Messe und Herrenmahl.* Arbeiten zur Kirchengeschichte, 8. Bonn: Marcus und Weber, 1926; 3d ed., Berlin: de Gruyter, 1955. English: *Mass and Lord's Supper.* Trans. D. H. G. Reeve. Leiden: Brill, 1953– . Translation of Lietzmann's book is complete in fascicle 4; fascicles 5–8 (1958–72) continue a supplementary essay by R. D. Richardson, "A Further Inquiry into Eucharistic Origins with Special Reference to New Testament Problems," begun in fascicle 4, pp. 217 ff.

———. "Der altchristliche Gottesdienst," reprinted in his *Kleine Schriften.* 3 vols. TU 67, 68, 74. Berlin: Akademie Verlag, 1958–1962. Vol. 3, pp. 28–42.

———. *Die Entstehung der christlichen Liturgie nach den ältesten Quellen.* Vorträge der Bibliothek Warburg 5 (1925/26). Reprinted ("Libelli," 100): Darmstadt: Wissenschaftliche Buchgesellschaft, 1963. Also reprinted in his *Kleine Schriften.* TU 74. Vol. 3, pp. 3–27.

CLARKE, WILLIAM KEMP LOWTHER. *Liturgy and Worship.* London: SPCK, 1932.

MICKLEM, NATHANIEL, ed. *Christian Worship: Studies in its History and Meaning.* Oxford: Oxford University Press, 1936.

MAXWELL, WILLIAM D. *An Outline of Christian Worship.* London: Oxford University Press, 1939. Reprinted 1963.

Dix, Gregory. *The Shape of the Liturgy.* London: Dacre, 1945; 4th ed., 1949; reprinted 1960.

Srawley, James Herbert. *The Early History of the Liturgy.* Cambridge Handbooks of Liturgical Study. Cambridge: Cambridge University Press, 1913; 2d ed., 1949.

Jungmann, Josef Andreas. *Missarum sollemnia.* 2 vols. Wien: Herder, 1948; 5th ed., 1962. English: *The Mass of the Roman Rite.* Trans. F. A. Brunner. New York: Benziger, 1951–55. 2d ed., revised and abridged; 1959 (1 vol.).

Stählin, H. "Die Geschichte des christlichen Gottesdienstes von der Urkirche bis zur Gegenwart." *Leiturgia* 1 (1954) : 1–81.

Nagel, William. *Geschichte des christlichen Gottesdienstes.* Sammlung Göschen 1202/2a. Berlin: de Gruyter, 1962; 2d ed., 1970.

Jones, B. H. "The Quest for the Origins of the Christian Liturgies." *Anglican Theological Review* 46 (1964) : 5–21.

Brunner, Peter. "Zur Lehre vom Gottesdienst der im Namen Jesu versammelten Gemeinde." *Leiturgia, Handbuch des evangelischen Gottesdienst* 1 (1954) : 83–361. English: *Worship in the Name of Jesus.* Trans. M. H. Bertram. St. Louis: Concordia, 1968.

Harrelson, Walter. *From Fertility Cult to Worship.* Garden City: Doubleday, 1969; Anchor Books, 1970. An assessment of the worship of ancient Israel.

Mendenhall, George E. "Biblical Faith and Cultic Evolution." *The Lutheran Quarterly* 5 (1953): 235–58.

Wengst, Klaus. *Christologische Formeln und Lieder des Urchristentums.* Studien zum Neuen Testament 7. Gütersloh: Gütersloher Verlagshaus Gerd Mohn, 1972.

Index of Scripture Passages

117